ELEMENTS

of

SUSHI

ELEMENTS
of
SUSHI

ELEMENTS

of

SUSHI

ELEMENTS

of

SUSHI

Author
Benjamin N. ChuChen

Project Manager
Anucha Praropkul

Project Coordinator
Cathy M. Fujimoto

Design and Layout
Yukari Ando, Advanced Digital Media, Inc.

Photographer
Kaz Majima, StudioKaz
(Except p3, p11, p115, p141)

Prop Stylist
Ellen Geerer
(p6, p7, p13, p14, p21, p25, p29, p33, p37, p41, p47, p51, p55,
p61, p67, p71, p75, p79, p83, p89, p93, p97, p99, p103, p105, p107)

Special contributions from:

Nobuhiro Tamura, Masahiko Tajima, Peter Han,

Anne Sena, Chet Douglass, Saori Minota, Kenneth Ishiki

Yumiyo Shiino, Kaori Toyoaki, and Kevin Barton.

Published in 2000 by Advanced Fresh Concepts Corporation
19205 S. Laurel Park Rd, Rancho Dominguez, CA 90220-6032

Library of Congress Cataloging-in-Publication Data is available
ISBN 0-9676101-0-9

Distributed by Advanced Fresh Concepts Corporation
19205 S. Laurel Park Rd, Rancho Dominguez, CA 90220-6032
Tel (310) 604-3200, Fax (310) 604-4900
www.afcsushi.com

Printed in Singapore

Foreword

Sushi is a healthy and nutritious food that can be enjoyed as a snack or a meal. The following pages are filled with facts about sushi and the fundamentals of sushi making. Large beautiful photographs and easy to follow step by step instructions take the fear out of making sushi and open the doors to a delightful culinary journey. Advanced Fresh Concepts Corporation (AFC) is pleased to share the basics of sushi making with the home cook. When AFC first introduced its line of Sushi Related Products, the tremendous response indicated that many people enjoyed making sushi at home. Based on this, AFC created the Ultimate Sushi Kit that incorporates all the products necessary for sushi making. To complement the sushi kit, AFC embarked on a project to teach our customers the proper techniques and to inspire them with more recipes. The result is "The Elements of Sushi". The ideas and recipes in these pages will make entertaining enjoyable for you and your guests. Use the basics illustrated in this book to create your own works of art! Enjoy and have fun!

Ryuji Ishii
President

Advanced Fresh Concepts Corporation

C O N T

E N T S

Introduction

"Irashaimase!"- a familiar phrase heard in all sushi bars means "Welcome!" Welcome to the exotic world of sushi! Many people equate sushi with raw fish and expect it to taste fishy or slippery. While it is true that some sushi are made with raw fish, many are made with vegetables or cooked seafood. Consuming raw foods, however, is not as foreign of a concept as you might think. Many people enjoy raw oysters or carpaccio (a raw beef appetizer offered in many Italian restaurants) without thinking twice. Eating raw fish may be intimidating at first but once you try it, you'll be hooked for life.

The purpose of this book is to introduce sushi - its origin, ingredients and cooking techniques. Also within these pages are easy recipes that will inspire the connoisseurs and open a whole new world of culinary delights to the novice. The secrets of good sushi are the rice, the freshness of the ingredients and the artistry in forming it. The easy to follow step by step instructions will illustrate how to wash and cook rice, roll and form sushi, and with some practice, you too will soon be making sushi similar to that in a sushi bar.

Sushi is quickly becoming part of mainstream America's diet as more and more Japanese restaurants and sushi bars open across the country. Many people have come to realize that not only is sushi delicious, it is also very healthy. Low in fat and high in protein, sushi is a convenient and rewarding alternative to fast foods. Nowadays, you can even find sushi at your local supermarket! So dive in and learn how to create the beautiful gem like packages of rice and seafood that is taking America by storm. Irashaimase!

Origin

"Sushi" is a specific style of Japanese cuisine that combines vinegar seasoned rice with a variety of seafood and vegetables. The word "sushi" actually means "vinegar rice". "Su" is the Japanese word for vinegar and "Shi" is an abbreviation of the word "Meshi", a colloquial name for cooked rice. When "sushi" follows a word ending in a vowel (ie. nigiri), it is pronounced "zushi" (nigiri zushi).

Sushi is believed to have its origin in Southeast Asian. People in this region used rice to preserve fish, a process later adopted by the Japanese. Layers of cleaned raw fish, salt and rice were pressed together in a jar and weighted with a stone. After a few weeks, the stone was removed and replaced with a lid. The rice and fish would then be left in the jar to ferment for up to a year. When the fish was ready to be eaten, it was removed from the jar and the rice was discarded. This original style of sushi is still available today at some restaurants in Tokyo.

Time passed and new methods of fermentation were invented to reduce the process to a few days. The Japanese discovered that the fermented rice had a sweet flavor and instead of discarding it as before, they ate it along with the fish. It was not until the 17th century, however, that the Japanese came up with the idea of adding vinegar to the rice to instantaneously achieve the fermented flavor and bypass the few days wait altogether. From this point on, two styles of sushi evolved - the Kansai style and the Edo style.

The Kansai style is named after the region where Osaka is presently located. Osaka was the center of commerce and the chefs there developed sushi that consisted of seasoned rice and other ingredients formed into decorative edible packages. Edo, the ancient name of Tokyo, was located on a bay abundant with fish and shellfish. Naturally, the sushi that developed in this area took the form of small pads of seasoned rice adorned with slices of raw seafood. A chef by the name of Yohei Hanaya in the early 1800's is credited with developing the Edo style which has evolved into the nigiri zushi we are familiar with today.

Landscape designed and photographed by Takendo Arii

SUSHI BAR SETTING

Unlike Americans, Japanese prefer to entertain their guests at restaurants and nightclubs. Many homes in Japan are small and few people have homes large enough to host guests. Even if one had a home large enough to seat guests comfortably, the preference is still a restaurant because in Japan, where humbleness is prized, inviting guests to one's home is considered pretentious. In a culture that dictates where people are to meet, restaurants and nightclubs fulfill this need by providing elegantly and lavishly decorated interiors for their patrons.

Sushi bars, especially the ones in Japan, are designed to create a comfortable environment for patrons to relax in and to enjoy the company of friends. Special attention is paid to keeping the sushi bar immaculate. Choose a sushi bar based on its décor, service and of course, its clientele. You can't go wrong if the majority of the clientele is Japanese.

A typical sushi bar setting will include the following dinnerware and condiments:

Geta

"Geta" is a traditional Japanese wooden shoe and because the plate that sushi is served on resembles the shoe, it is also called a geta. The geta is often situated on a ledge between the chef and the customer and within arms reach of the chef. After the chef prepares the order of sushi, he places it on the geta. The customer is then welcomed to pick up the sushi with either his fingers or chopsticks. Leave the geta on the ledge; do not bring it down in front of you or else the chef will have no where to place your next order of sushi.

Chopsticks

Disposable chopsticks, or "ohashi" in Japanese, are available at each sushi bar. They are generally made of bamboo or willow and are sealed in a paper wrapping to show that they have never been used before. Chopsticks come in several shapes and sizes and are used to eat sashimi or other appetizers before the sushi meal. Sushi itself can be eaten with chopsticks but most connoisseurs prefer using their fingers.

Hand Towel

Since sushi is eaten with the fingers, the waiter/waitress will give you an "oshibori", a small hand towel, to clean your hands with before you start your meal. This towel can be very hot so be careful when wiping your hands. After using the towel, the proper etiquette is to fold it neatly and put it to one side. During the course of the meal, you may need to use it on more than one occasion. Just remember to fold the towel again neatly after using it. If you are serving sushi at home and want to provide the full experience of a sushi bar for your guests, heat the damp towels in the microwave for 1-2 minutes.

Soy Sauce

Soy sauce is to sushi as ketchup is to hot dogs. It's just not the same without it! Enjoying sushi is to taste the distinct flavors of the fish, rice, wasabi, and of course, soy sauce. In Japan, soy sauce is called "shoyu" and like all other soy sauces in Asia, the main ingredient is

soybean. Salt and yeast are added to the soybeans and the mixture is allowed to age for several months. The fermentation process produces a dark brown liquid, which is then bottled.

There are many types of soy sauces and each type is distinguished by the ingredients added to the soybeans during the fermentation process. Most soy sauces are made from a mixture of soybean and wheat in varying proportions, but some are also made with mushrooms instead of wheat. There is a category of soy sauce in Japan called "tamari" that is primarily brewed with soybeans and little or no wheat. The absence of wheat results in an enzymatic reaction rather than an alcoholic fermentation during the brewing process which produces a soy sauce that is extremely smooth and rich in aroma.

Many sushi bars offer shoyu and reduced sodium soy sauces but if they have tamari available, you should definitely give it a try. Chances are you will prefer the taste over the other varieties. Not all soy sauces are the same! In addition to tamari, there are other types brewed especially for sushi and sashimi. Your local Asian grocery store should carry a variety of soy sauces.

Green Tea

Green tea is the most common type of tea in Japan and is often served with sushi. Sipping this drink between servings of sushi helps to refresh the palate and prepare your taste buds for the next presentation. Along with black tea, oolong tea and three thousand other varieties, green tea comes from the Camellia Sinensis plant. Only the buds and the young leaves are harvested and used to develop different types of teas. Herbal teas such as chamomile, however, are not from the Camellia Sinensis plant. In fact, herbal teas are properly known as infusions and use leaves, flowers and other dried ingredients from various plants.

Tea is processed in four stages after the leaves are harvested. First, the leaves are allowed to wilt for several hours. This process reduces the moisture content of the leaves and is crucial in producing black tea, but this step is often omitted in green tea production. The next stage is

steaming or pan firing. The tea leaves are exposed to a high heat source that destroys the enzymes that lead to fermentation. This process prevents oxidation and keeps the leaves green, hence the name. In black tea production, the leaves are allowed to ferment. The third stage of production involves rolling the leaves to give them their appearance. High quality teas have tightly rolled leaves. The final stage of production involves firing the leaves. This last step ensures that the leaves are thoroughly dried and that oxidation will not occur.

There are many health benefits associated with green tea. Studies have shown that green tea not only reduces cholesterol levels but also protects against some forms of cancer. These properties are attributed to a powerful antioxidant called polyphenol found in the leaves. Antioxidants protect the body against free radicals believed to be the cause of cancer and heart disease.

Ginger

Sushi is always served with a small amount of pickled ginger or "gari", on the side. The ginger is sliced paper thin and marinated in a vinegar solution to give a refreshing and unique flavor. Eating a piece of gari will freshen the mouth and erase the flavors of the previous piece of sushi so that the palate can distinguish and enjoy the next piece of sushi. Gari is intended to cleanse the palate and not to be eaten as a side dish; so don't feel obligated to eat all the gari the chef gives you.

Edamame

After you have cleaned your hands with the hot towel, the waiter/waitress will serve you a small dish of soybeans or "edamame". The soybeans have been blanched in salted water and make a refreshing appetizer. To eat the soybeans, simply squeeze the beans from the pod into your mouth. A crisp cold beer is a nice accompaniment to the soybeans.

Sake/Beer

Although green tea is served with the sushi meal, many people choose to order sake or beer in addition to the tea. The sushi bar has become a venue for entertaining and relaxing with friends, and what better way to socialize than over a glass of beer or sake. Sake is a wine made from rice and is served hot or cold. When you order sake, the waiter/waitress will bring it to you in a porcelain vessel along with several tiny cups resembling shot glasses. Pour the sake into the cups and toast your friends with a fervent "Kanpai!", which means, "Bottoms Up!" You may want to offer this drink to your sushi chef as well. Most chefs will be more than happy to accept the toast and share in the revelry. Sushi bars can be rather loud and entertaining especially when the patrons and chefs have had a couple shots of sake.

Wasabi

If you've tried wasabi before, whether intentionally or unknowingly, you will never forget the spicy flavor of this condiment. Although the flavor is strong, the spiciness dissipates almost immediately unlike that of chili peppers that leave a burning sensation in your mouth for what may seem like an eternity. Wasabi is always served with sushi and it completes a quartet of flavors along with the fish, soy sauce and vinegar flavored rice.

Wasabi is a plant native to Japan. It has such specific growth requirements that it can only flourish in areas where the spring water is fresh and slightly alkaline. The temperature of the water must also remain between 48°- 54°F. In the summer, the plant requires shade and in the winter, it needs direct sunlight. Even under favorable conditions, the wasabi plant takes 2-3 years to mature. Its long cultivation and stringent growth environment make it an expensive and highly sought after commodity.

Wasabi is made from the root of the plant and can be purchased in a freshly grated form or in powder form. Many brands of powdered wasabi however, include a mixture of horseradish, mustard and food coloring. Wasabi is a great source of vitamin C. The amount of vitamin C in 2.5 grams of wasabi is equivalent to that of 3 oranges. Its unique properties also allow it to remove odors from raw fish and prevent the growth of bacteria. Perhaps these were some reasons why wasabi was first served with sushi and sashimi.

Sushi Bar Etiquette

There is no set order of eating the various kinds of nigiri zushi. Many Japanese begin with maguro (tuna) and follow it with whatever strikes their fancy. If you are not familiar with sushi, you may want to ask the chef for his recommendation. Even experienced diners seek the chef's advice for the best selections. If you order a combination sushi plate, always eat the pieces wrapped with nori (seaweed) first. The reason behind this is that the crisp nori becomes soggy after prolong contact with the damp rice. So, to enjoy the flavor and texture of the nori, eat hand rolls and gunkan sushi first.

The proper way of eating sushi is to pick it up with your fingers and eat it in one bite. Connoisseurs in Japan will pick up a piece of sushi, dip it into the soy sauce and transfer it to their mouths in one motion. You should never bite half of it and leave the other half on the plate - it is considered bad manners to do so. Sushi in Japan is made with a smaller portion of rice and can fit easily into the mouth. In America, however, eating sushi in one bite may be more of a challenge because a larger amount of rice is used. If you are uncomfortable using your fingers, don't worry - that's what the chopsticks are for. The sushi bars in America will provide disposable wooden chopsticks for your use. Using chopsticks is a tell tale sign of a novice sushi diner but since the majority of the patrons in American sushi bars use chopsticks, you'll fit in perfectly.

If using chopsticks is too difficult, feel free to use your hands. You will give the impression that you're a connoisseur.

1. Pick up the piece of nigiri zushi with you thumb, index and middle finger.

2. Dip the end of the topping into the soy sauce and place the sushi into your mouth so that the topping is the first ingredient to touch the tongue.

If you have never used chopsticks before, you may just want to use your fingers. Learning to use chopsticks takes some practice but once you have mastered it, it's almost second nature. The chopsticks in the sushi bars come sheathed in a paper wrapper and are joined at the top. Remove the wrapper and carefully split them apart. Follow the directions below on how to use these very unique eating utensils.

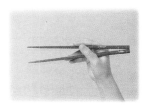

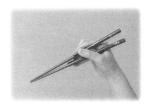

1. Place one chopstick in the hollow between your thumb and index finger and let it rest on the tip of your ring finger.

2. Rest the other chopstick on the tip of your middle finger and the edge of your index finger. With your thumb, hold the chopstick in place.

3. The correct position to hold the chopsticks is about three quarters of the way towards the end of the chopstick.

4. To pick up food, pivot the top chopstick up and down with your index and middle fingers while using your thumb to hold it in place. Keep the bottom chopstick stationary at all times.

5. The two chopsticks should act like a pair of pincers to grab food.

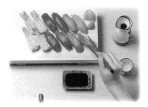

6. To eat sushi with chopsticks, pick up the piece of sushi between your chopsticks.

7. Turn the piece of sushi on its side gently to keep the rice from falling apart.

8. Pick up the sushi with your chopsticks and bring it to the dish of soy sauce.

9. Dip the end of the topping into the soy sauce and bring the piece of sushi to your mouth.

Now that you have mastered eating sushi with chopsticks and your fingers, there is just one more thing to keep in mind. When dipping sushi into the soy sauce, be sure to dip just the end of the topping. Do not drown your sushi in it. Not only will you get a mouthful of soy sauce, you run the risk of the rice falling apart in your soy sauce dish, making it even more difficult to use your chopsticks. The idea is to taste the different flavors of the vinegared rice, the topping and the soy sauce. If you overload on the soy sauce, basically all you will taste is the soy sauce.

Rice

Rice is the main ingredient and foundation of sushi. If the rice is not perfectly prepared, even though the other ingredients are of the highest quality, the sushi is considered ruined. Apprentices in sushi bars spend years learning proper rice cooking techniques before they graduate to other skills. Even more important than the cooking technique is the choice of rice. Sushi chefs are very particular about the kind of rice they use and will often have rice merchants mix a special blend of rice specifically for their restaurant.

Sushi bars in Japan almost always use short grain white rice. The moist and sticky properties of the rice are essential in forming the sushi into various shapes. Long grain rice or the instant rice we are accustomed to in America should be avoided at all cost. These types of rice cannot provide the appearance or texture needed for sushi preparation. If short grain white rice is not available, a medium grain will work just as well. For those who are more health conscious, brown rice can also be a substitute. If brown rice is used, do not flavor it with the vinegar dressing (awasezu) as the rice may result in an unpleasant taste.

Water

The quality of the water is just as important to the sushi chef as the type of rice. Many sushi chefs are very selective of the water they use because it plays such an integral part in sushi making. Water is used to rinse, soak and cook the rice and the chefs believe that the contact the water has with the rice will affect the taste of the cooked product. Some chefs will only use mountain spring water while others ionize their water. There are even chefs who store the water overnight in a large covered vat before using it. This water that has been hidden from the light is called "still water".

Awasezu

The vinegar dressing used to flavor the rice is called "awazesu". There are many recipes that differ slightly in the amounts of ingredients used but the basic components are rice vinegar, salt and sugar. When blending awasezu, use only rice vinegar as other types of vinegar are too strong in flavor.

The vinegar in awasezu prevents rice from spoiling and together with salt and sugar adds a delicate flavor to the rice. The awasezu should be well balanced and vinegar should not be too overpowering that it masks the subtle flavors of the sugar and salt. A well flavored rice testifies to the skillfulness of the chef and distinguishes great sushi from good sushi.

Nori

Nori is roasted seaweed, and it is used to wrap each piece of sushi. As one of the main ingredients in sushi, the chefs pay special attention to the type of Nori they use. Nori is a blend of 20 species of Porphyra algae that are cultivated in nitrogen rich sea water between November and April. The highest quality nori is black in color. Since black nori is expensive, a lesser quality green nori is also available. The green color is derived from mixing other species of seaweed in with the Porphyra algae. Nori is very nutritious with high levels of protein, vitamins (A, B1, B2, B6, Niacin and C) and trace minerals.

ELEMENTS OF SUSHI

Styles of Sushi

There are two traditions of sushi making - the Kansai tradition and the Edo tradition. Exemplifying the Kansai tradition is oshi zushi, a style of sushi made by using a wooden mold to press rice and other ingredients into a square or rectangular shape. The sushi is then cut into smaller sections. Chirashi zushi is also from the Kansai tradition. In chirashi zushi, seafood and vegetables are sliced into pieces and arranged on top of a bed of rice. Kansai styles are differentiated from Edo styles by the use of more cooked ingredients than raw ones.

In America, we are familiar with styles of sushi from the Edo Tradition. The two main styles are maki zushi and nigiri zushi. Maki means "rolled" and the chef uses a bamboo mat to roll a sheet of toasted seaweed together with rice, fish and vegetables. The California Roll is the most popular maki zushi. The type of sushi you are most likely served when you sit at the sushi bar is nigiri zushi. Nigiri means "squeezed" and the chef uses his hand to gently form the rice into an oval shape. He then finishes the sushi by placing a slice of seafood on top. Most of the toppings are different varieties of raw fish but some very popular ones such as shrimp, egg and eel are cooked.

Whether you prefer cooked or raw ingredients, there is a type of sushi for you. If you are a novice, start with cooked items such as California Roll or shrimp nigiri. As you become more adventurous, try some of the fish items such as tuna or salmon. The following pages will show you the basics of sushi making from California Rolls to nigiri zushi. Use the recipes listed in this book to make healthy, delicious and attractive meals or as a guide to your own original creations. Once you've learned the basics, you can use any ingredients you want to create a meal that will amaze your family and friends.

GIANT ROLL

Giant Roll

"Maki" means rolled. Any type of sushi that has rice and nori wrapped around other ingredients is considered maki zushi. The varieties of ingredients used as the fillings for this type of sushi are endless. Vegetables and seafood are traditionally used. The vegetables are either fresh or pickled and the seafood can be raw or cooked. Use any ingredient you like - you are only limited by your imagination.

The foundation of maki zushi is vinegar-seasoned rice on a sheet of roasted seaweed. Slices of seafood and vegetables are layered on top. The rice, nori and filling ingredients are then rolled together into a cylindrical shape with a bamboo mat called "makisu". A makisu is essential in successfully shaping the sushi into a roll. You will find it extremely difficult to get the desired shape if you don't have a makisu.

The "giant roll", or "Futomaki" in Japanese, is the largest of the three categories of maki zushi. It consists of four to six filling ingredients and uses a whole sheet of nori. The other types of maki zushi are "Hosomaki" or "small roll", made with half a sheet of nori and usually just one filling ingredient, and "Chumaki" or "medium roll", consisting of two to three ingredients. Most restaurants prefer to use this size for their California Rolls.

The California Roll is the most famous of all maki zushi. Even people who are not familiar with sushi may have heard of it. Although most restaurants prefer to serve it in the medium roll form, it is also available in the giant roll category. The California Roll, however, is not even Japanese - it's as American as apple pie! Created by chefs in California, its popularity is the result of familiar ingredients such as cucumber, avocado and imitation crab. It has such universal appeal that even sushi bars in Japan now offer this item!

Giant California Roll

Giant California Roll

Before making maki zushi, there are several items you will need to prepare. You will need a bowl of tezu (water mixed with several teaspoons of rice vinegar) to wet your hands to keep the rice from sticking to them. Next, wrap the makisu with saran wrap or plastic film. The saran wrap will keep the rice from sticking to the makisu and will make it easier to clean afterwards. Have a sharp knife ready to slice the sushi into smaller pieces when you have finished rolling it. Avoid using a serrated blade as it will tear the nori and leave the sushi with jagged edges, compromising the presentation.

Whether you are making Futomaki, Chumaki or Hosomaki, always remember to position the makisu horizontally so that it can be rolled away from you. Place a sheet of nori on the makisu with the longer edge flush against the base of the makisu. Each piece of nori has a shiny side and a rough side; place the nori on the makisu with the rough side facing up. Before handling the rice, dip your fingers into the tezu and moisten both hands.

Giant California Roll

Sushi rice	1 1/4 cup
Nori (roasted seaweed)	1 sheet
Cucumber	1 strip (8" x 3/8" x 3/8")
Avocado	3 slices (1/4" thick)
Imitation crab	1 strip

Makes 8 pieces

1. Place 1 1/4 cup of sushi rice on the rough side of the nori.

2. With your fingers, spread the rice neatly and evenly over the nori leaving 1/2 inch uncovered along the far side. Spread the rice gingerly over the nori. Do not press the rice so hard that you crush the rice grains.

3. Line the center of the rice with a row of imitation crab followed by a row of cucumber next to it. The cucumber can be cut into strips about the same size as the imitation crab or shredded using a mandolin. Finally, add 2-3 slices of avocado on top.

4. Roll the sushi by picking up the edge of the makisu nearest to you with your thumbs and forefingers.

5. Lift the makisu and roll the nori away from you. Use your fingers from both hands to hold the ingredients in place as you roll the sushi forward.

6. Roll the nori once so that the rice from the near side and far side meet, leaving the 1/2 inch of nori open.

7. Lift the leading edge of the makisu and roll the sushi forward once more so that the uncovered portion of nori is now joined with the rest of the roll.

8. Grip the makisu with both hands at the center and then move to the two ends in 2-3 grips. Pressing the sushi firmly together with your hands will help maintain its shape and keep the rice and nori from unraveling. If some of the fillings have popped out at the ends during the rolling process, push them back in or discard them when you cut the sushi roll.

9. Use a sharp knife and cut the roll in half. Cut through the sushi in one swift motion; do not saw back and forth.

10. To prevent the rice from sticking to the knife and to ensure a smooth cut, wet the blade with water or a damp cloth.

11. Place both halves side by side and cut into quarters. You may discard the end pieces if they look uneven or if the ingredients have popped out.

Inari Roll

Sushi rice	1/2 cup
Carrots	1 Tablespoon (finely diced)
Inari	2 pieces (cut open)
Eel	1 strip (4" x 1/2" x 1/2")
Omelet (pg.126)	1 strip (4" x 1/2" x 1/2")
Cucumber	1 strip (4" x 3/8" x 3/8")
Mitsuba	3 pieces
Radish sprouts	For garnish

Makes 3 pieces

The rolling technique is the same as the Giant California Roll. Instead of using nori as the base, this recipe calls for inari (fried tofu pockets). Slice open the two shorter ends of the inari to form a larger sheet. Place two sheets of inari together so that one side is overlapping. Combine the carrots and rice together and spread it over the inari sheets. Next, layer the eel, omelet, and cucumber on top of the rice. Roll the inari as you would a Giant California Roll and secure it with pieces of mitsuba (a Japanese vegetable similar to cilantro). Cut the roll into three pieces.

Futomaki

Sushi rice	11/4 cup
Nori (roasted seaweed)	1 sheet
Denbu (fish powder)	1 tsp.
Omelet	1 strip (8" x 1/2" x 1/2")
Kampyo (dried gourd)	4 strips
Shiitake mushrooms	1 Tbsp.
Spinach	4 leaves (par boiled)

Makes 8 pieces

Although Futomaki means "large roll", it is also the name of this particular type of sushi. The instruction for making Futomaki is the same as the Giant California Roll; the only difference is the ingredients. Spread rice onto the nori, leaving 1/2" at the far edge. Sprinkle the denbu along the center of the rice and line the rest of the ingredients next to the denbu. Use the makisu to roll the nori and other ingredients together. Cut into 8 pieces.

MEDIUM ROLL

Medium Roll

In addition to the large Futomaki, you can make a smaller size roll by using half a sheet of nori. This smaller size roll is called Chumaki or medium roll. Most sushi bars distinguish this type of roll from Futomaki and Hosomaki by flipping the roll "inside-out" so that the rice is on the outside instead of the nori. California Rolls are often served in this fashion.

Medium rolls usually have 2-3 filling ingredients. If you add more than 3 fillings, the roll will be too thick and you will not be able to form it properly. There are many varieties of medium rolls; a popular one is the Orange Roll. It is a basic California Roll with masago (smelt roe) on the outside.

The recipes in this book are designed to show you the basics of each type of rolls. You can follow them or use them as a springboard to create your own original recipes. Vary the filling ingredients and use your favorite items. The assortments of sushi that you can come up with are endless. Roasted chicken, teriyaki beef or even tuna salad will work well.

Spicy Tuna Roll

Spicy Tuna Roll

Spicy Tuna

Sushi rice	1/2 cup
Nori (roasted seaweed)	1/2 sheet
Tuna	1 strip (8" x 1/2" x 1/2")
Cucumber	1 strip (8" x 1/2" x 1/2")
Sesame seeds	For garnish

Spicy Sauce

Mayonnaise	16 tsp.
Chili sauce	4 tsp.
Chili oil	1 tsp.

For a spicier sauce, add more chili sauce

Makes 8 pieces

1. Place 1/2 a sheet of nori on the makisu with the longer edge flush against the base of the makisu.

2. Spread 1/2 cup of rice over the nori covering the whole sheet.

As with making any type of sushi, prepare a bowl of tezu and wrap the makisu in saran wrap. The tezu will keep the rice from sticking to your hands and the saran wrap will make cleanup much easier. The rolling technique is the same as the Giant California Roll, so once you've mastered it, you can make any size of maki zushi you like.

3. Sprinkle sesame seeds evenly over the rice and flip the nori over so that the rice side is facing down and the seaweed side is now on top.

4. Line the center of the nori with a strip of tuna. Next to it, place a strip of cucumber. To achieve the symmetrical presentation seen in the picture on the previous page, cut the cucumber and tuna into the same length, width and height. Spoon in a line of spicy sauce. An easy way of applying the spicy sauce is to use a squeeze bottle to dispense it.

5. Lift the makisu and roll the sushi away from you. As with the Giant California Roll, use your fingers to hold the filling in place as you form the sushi.

6. Roll the sushi in one swift motion, leaving about 1/2 inch of nori at the far end. With both hands still holding onto the makisu, firmly press the nori, rice and ingredients together.

7. Lift the top edge of the makisu and roll the sushi over once more so that the 1/2 inch of nori is now joined with the rest of the roll.

8. Grip the roll and firmly squeeze it along its length to tighten it. Use a sharp knife and cut the roll in half. Place both halves side by side and cut into quarters. You should have 8 equal size pieces.

Orange Roll

Sushi rice	1/2 cup
Nori (roasted seaweed)	1/2 sheet
Imitation crab	1 stick (cut 1/2 lengthwise)
Cucumber	8-10 julienne strips
Avocado	2 wedges (1/4 - 1/2" thick)
Masago (capelin roe)	2 Tbsp.

Makes 8 pieces

Spread 1/2 cup of rice over the nori just as you did with the Spicy Roll. Instead of sprinkling sesame seeds, spread 2 Tbsp. of masago over the rice. Layer in the filling ingredients and use the makisu to roll the sushi. Another method is to make the roll and then spoon on the masago as pictured above. Cut into 8 pieces.

Dragon Roll

Sushi rice	1/2 cup
Nori (roasted seaweed)	1/2 sheet
Eel	1 strip (8" x 1/2" x 1/2")
Avocado	8-10 slices (1/8" thick)
Cucumber	8-10 julienne strips
Eel sauce	Drizzle on top

Makes 8 pieces

The Dragon Roll, with its bright green and yellow colors, is definitely eye catching. Use the same techniques as the Spicy Roll to form the base of rice and nori. Line the eel and cucumber along the center and roll the sushi together. After you have shaped it, place the slices of avocado on top. Overlap the avocado so that the rice on the bottom does not shows through. Place the makisu over the completed roll and gently squeeze to shape it one more time.

SMALL ROLL

Small Roll

Hosomaki is the smallest of the maki zushi. Only three ingredients are used, rice, nori and a filling ingredient. In Japan, the traditional Hosomaki ingredients are kampyo (dried gourd), tuna and cucumber, but you can use any ingredient you like - just remember to limit the filling to one ingredient. Hosomaki are delightful tiny gem like packages that are eaten with the hands. Their simplicity makes an attractive presentation especially when time is taken to carefully prepare them. When making Hosomaki, as with all the other types of maki zushi, try to keep an even amount of rice around the filling. If you can, try to use the same amount of filling for all your Hosomaki so that each piece will look the same. Experiment by cutting the fillings into different geometric shapes or using fillings with different colors to create eye-catching hors d'oeuvres.

Tuna Roll

Tuna Roll

Sushi rice	1/3 cup
Nori (roasted seaweed)	1/2 sheet
Tuna	1 strip (8" x 1/2" x 1/2")

Makes 8 pieces

1. Place a sheet of nori on the makisu. Make sure that the rough side of the nori is facing you and the longer edge is flush against the base of the makisu.

2. Cover the nori with rice, leaving 1/2 inch of nori uncovered along the far side.

3. Place a strip of tuna in the center of the rice.

4. Lift the makisu and roll the rice and nori over once.

5. As you roll the nori, you may need to use your fingers to hold the tuna in place.

6. Complete the first roll by bringing the edges of the rice together. You should still have the 1/2 inch of bare nori left. Press the roll gently to form the shape.

7. Lift the top of the makisu and roll the sushi over once more to join the strip of nori to the rest of the sushi.

8. Once again, press all around the makisu to tighten and shape the roll. Cut the roll into 8 pieces.

NIGIRI

Nigiri Zushi

Nigiri is by far the most artistic form of sushi. The bright colors and patterns of the different varieties of seafood create a visual smorgasbord that is almost too beautiful to eat. Nigiri is the type of sushi served most often at the sushi bar. When you place an order for tuna, salmon or any other type of seafood, the chef quickly and skillfully molds the rice into a small block and lays a piece of sliced fish over it. Nigiri zushi is always served in pairs and each piece should be just large enough to eat in one bite.

Nigiri in Japanese means "squeezed" and is appropriately used to distinguish this type of sushi from maki zushi or "rolled" sushi. The chef gently squeezes a small amount of rice into a block shape and presses a piece of fish or shellfish over the rice. This is done with remarkable speed and the chef is usually able to prepare a pair of nigiri within seconds of ordering. A choice piece of topping should be approximately 1/4 inch in thickness and drape over both ends of the rice pad covering a majority of the surface area.

The toppings used in nigiri zushi are usually slices of raw fish, shellfish and roe but there are also a variety of cooked toppings such as shrimp, egg and eel. Nigiri is so simple in composition that the topping must be at its peak to deliver the best flavor. Only the premium cuts of fish and the freshest seafood are used for nigiri, justifying the high price for each order. Many sushi bars import fish directly from Japan and some even maintain live shellfish, such as clams and sea urchins, in aquariums preparing them only when customers place an order. Now, that is fresh!

Nigiri Combination

Nigiri

Sushi Rice	1 cup
Tuna	1 slice
Snapper	1 slice
Salmon	1 slice
Spotted sardine	1 slice
Ikura	1 slice
Octopus	1 slice
Eel	1 slice
Cooked shrimp	1 piece

Garnish:

      Green onion chopped

      Eel sauce

Makes 8 pieces

Mold the rice into small blocks approximately 2 1/2" X 1" X 1". The type of seafood pictured on the previous page is listed above but you can use any topping you desire.

Before making nigiri zushi, you should have a bowl of tezu handy to moisten your hand to keep the rice from sticking to them. The fish you are planning to use should already be sliced and the wasabi should be ready to use as well. Wasabi usually comes in a powder form and requires a small amount of water to make it into a paste. You can also find freshly grated wasabi packaged in a tube at your local Asian market.

1. Wet your left palm by dipping your right fingertips into the tezu and wiping the liquid onto the palm.

2. Repeat with the other hand. Both palms should be moist before picking up the rice and fish.

3. With your right hand, scoop up a golf ball size of rice and gently squeeze it into a block by cupping your fingers and palm together.

4. Gently shape the rice on both sides using your left thumb and index finger. It should now resemble a rectangular block.

5. Pick up the topping with the left hand by holding the upper end of the topping between the thumb and index finger and allow it to rest in the joints of the fingers. While holding the ball of rice, use your right index finger to smear a small amount of wasabi onto the center of the topping.

6. Place the block of rice on top of the topping.

7. Cup your left hand and with the left thumb, press the fish and rice together.

8. Press the top of the rice with your right index finger to flatten out the top.

9. Use your right thumb and index finger to grasp onto the piece of sushi and turn it over so that the fish portion is now facing up.

10. Simultaneously squeeze and press the sushi with your left hand and right index finger to shape it.

11. Pick up the sushi between your right thumb and index finger and turn the sushi around 180° so that the two ends are now reversed. Slightly tilt your left hand downwards so that the fingers wrap snugly around the piece of sushi. Repeat the previous steps by gently squeezing the sushi with your left hand and right index finger.

12. You should now have a well-shaped piece of nigiri zushi. If the sushi requires more shaping, press and squeeze it again to get the desired shape.

Squid Nigiri

Sushi rice   1 oz
Squid   1 slice (3" x 1 1/2" x 1/4")
Nori (roasted seaweed)   2 strips (3" x 1/8 ")

Makes 1 piece

To make squid nigiri, mold the rice into a small block and place a piece of squid on top. Score the squid 2-3 times to tenderize and create an interesting pattern. Wrap a strip of nori around the finished sushi as a garnish.

Tamago Nigiri

Sushi rice   1 oz.
Nori (roasted seaweed)   1 strips (3" x 1/2")
Omelet   1 pieces (3' x 1" x 1/2")

Makes 1 piece

Prepare the piece of omelet ahead of time and place it on top of the rice after you have molded the rice into the proper shape and size. Directions for preparing the omelet is on page 126. Wrap the nori around the finished sushi and secure it with a grain of rice.

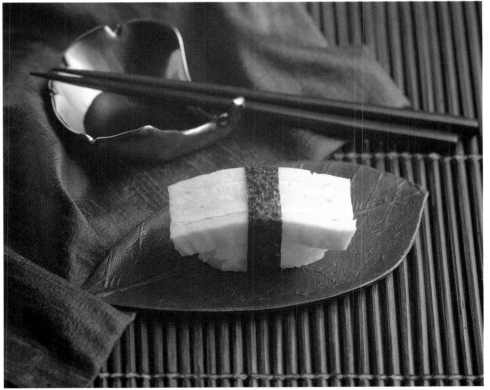

GUNKAN

Gunkan Sushi

Gunkan means "battleship" in Japanese and lends its namesake to this type of sushi. It is a style of nigiri zushi developed for the purpose of keeping formless ingredients on top of the rice. When the rice is wrapped with a wide piece of nori and adorned with colorful toppings, it does somewhat resembles a battleship.

Some favorite nigiri toppings such as capelin roe (masago), salmon roe (ikura), and sea urchin (uni) will not stay on top of the rice because of their consistency and require the aid of a piece of seaweed to secure them in place. To make gunkan sushi, wrap a piece of toasted seaweed or nori around a block of rice. Form the block of rice following the procedures for making nigiri zushi and then wrap the piece of nori around it to create a barrel shape. The width of the nori is taller than the sides of the rice forming a cavity to hold the toppings. With a spoon, fill the cavity with the desired topping.

Gunkan sushi is customarily served in pairs at sushi bars but at home, how you serve gunkan is at your discretion. You may want to serve a piece of each type of gunkan (as pictured on the right) to give your guests an assortment of flavors. Gunkan sushi is not limited to the toppings pictured; use this method of sushi preparation for any topping that will not remain steady on top of the rice.

Gunkan Combination

Gunkan

Sushi rice	3 oz.
Nori (roasted seaweed)	3 strips (1" x 6")
Ikura (salmon roe)	1 Tbsp.
Uni (sea urchin)	1 Tbsp.
Masago (capelin roe)	1 Tbsp.
Quail egg	1 egg
Cucumber	3 pieces - sliced paper thin

Makes 3 pieces

After molding the rice into the proper nigiri size, wrap a piece of nori around it. Secure the nori by using a crushed rice grain as an adhesive. Spoon in the ikura, uni or masago. To garnish the uni, cut paper thin slices of cucumbers and place them into the sushi before adding the uni. For the masago sushi, separate the yolk from the quail egg and add on top of the sushi just before serving.

1. Cut the nori into 1 inch wide by 6 inches long strips. With a wet hand, mold a golf ball size of rice into an oblong shape. If desired, spread a small amount of wasabi on top of the rice.

2. Pick up a piece of nori and press it to the side of the rice ball. Nori is like paper and will wilt when it comes in contact with water. So, make sure that the hand you use to pick up the nori is dry. Wrap the nori around the rice so that the rice forms the bottom of the sushi. As the nori is taller than the rice, you should now have an empty cavity to place the topping in.

3. Spoon the desired topping into the sushi.

HAND ROLL

Hand Roll

Hand rolls are the cone-shaped sushi people order at the sushi bar. The Japanese name for hand roll is "temaki zushi" and like maki zushi, you can use any filling you like. This type of sushi is the easiest to make at home. All you have to do is to roll the nori and ingredients into a cone shape. The hand roll is designed to fit comfortably in your hand, hence the name and should be eaten with the hands. No chopsticks required!

For best results, eat the hand rolls immediately. The contrast of the crisp nori with the rice and other filling ingredients is the uniqueness of this type of sushi. When left sitting on a platter for an extended period of time, the nori absorbs moisture from the rice and becomes soggy.

Sushi-making parties are fun and exciting ways to entertain friends. Show your friends how to make hand rolls and let them create their own versions by providing an assortment of ingredients. Prepare the rice and filling ingredients ahead of time and then watch everyone enjoy him or herself making and eating hand rolls.

Hand Roll Combination

Hand Rolls

Grilled Salmon Hand Roll

Sushi rice	1/2 cup
Nori (roasted seaweed)	1/2 sheet
Green leaf lettuce	1 small leaf
Grilled salmon	1 piece (1" x 4" x 1/2")
Green onion	3" stalk thinly sliced
Yamagobo (mountain burdock)	2 strips
Cucumber	5-7 julienne strips

Shrimp Tempura Hand Roll

Sushi rice	1/2 cup
Nori (roasted seaweed)	1/2 sheet
Shrimp tempura	1 piece
Masago (capelin roe)	1 tsp.
Cucumber	5-7 julienne strips
Radish sprouts	For garnish

Makes 2 hand rolls

Hand rolls are quick and easy to make. After spreading the rice onto the nori, place the fillings into the center of the rice and roll the nori into a cone shape. Secure the nori with a piece of rice. You may be able to find shrimp tempura at your local grocery store. If your supermarket does not carry prepared shrimp tempura, purchase a box of tempura batter and follow the instructions on the box. Fry the shrimp tempura before you begin making hand rolls.

1. Use 1/2 a sheet of nori per hand roll. Place the piece of nori on your left hand with the rough side facing up.

2. Spread 1/2 a cup on rice on the left side of the nori in a fan shape. Press the rice down in the center to make a groove for the filling. If you like, you can spread a small amount of wasabi on the rice.

3. Place the fillings of your choice on top of the rice.

4. Start with the bottom left corner of the nori and fold it towards the upper right corner, forming a pointed end.

5. Roll the nori over once more to form a cone shape. If you find that the nori is not sticking to the cone, use a rice grain as an adhesive to seal the roll.

INARI

Inari Zushi

Inari are deep-fried tofu pockets stuffed with vinegar-seasoned rice. In Japanese folklore, foxes are the messengers for Inari, the god of grains. No one is sure why this type of sushi is called inari; it may be because the shape of the tofu pockets resembles the pointed ears of the fox.

In America, inari zushi is often called a "football" because of its resemblance to the pigskin. The sweet and savory flavor of the inari has delighted many palates and since raw fish is not part of the ingredients, it is often the first step for many people exploring sushi. Sushi veterans also enjoy inari and it is one of the most popular types of sushi in the United States as well as Japan.

Inari is available in most Asian grocery stores. They are often pre-sliced to make it easier for the consumer to use. The same seasoned rice used in sushi is also used as the filling for the inari. Some people prefer to add sesame seeds or other kinds of seasonings to the rice before using it to stuff the tofu pockets.

Basic Inari Zushi

Inari

Sushi rice	1 cup
Inari	4 bags
Sesame seeds	Optional

Makes 4 pieces

Inari is a quick and delicious snack or a light lunch. Measure 1/4 cup (approximately 2 oz.) of rice for each piece of inari. Stuff the rice into the pockets and fold the ends over to cover the rice. Place the inari with the seam side down. Some people prefer to add sesame seeds to the inari. This is optional.

1. If the inari you buy is already pre-sliced, start making this simple sushi by filling it with rice. Inari that is not pre-sliced is usually rectangular in shape. All you need to do is to cut each piece in half and open the center of each piece to make a pouch.

2. Fill the tofu pouch loosely with rice. Do not over stuff the pouch as it may break. The amount of rice used should be about 1/2 - 3/4 volume of the pouch. Sprinkle sesame seeds onto the rice at this point if you plan to add more flavor to the inari.

3. Wrap the edges over the rice to seal the pouch.

4. Position the inari with the seam down to keep the rice from spilling out.

4 Color Inari

Sushi rice	1 cup
Inari	8 bags
Omelet	8 tsp. minced
Pickled Cucumber	8 tsp. minced
Carrot	8 tsp. minced
Ground chicken (cooked)	8 tsp. minced

Ground chicken preparation

Ground chicken	1/2 lb.
Soy sauce	2 tsp.
Cooking oil	2 Tbsp.
Salt and pepper	Dash

Makes 8 pieces

Brown 1/2 lb. of ground chicken in 2 tablespoons of cooking oil. Add a dash of salt and pepper and thoroughly cook the chicken. After the chicken is cooked, stir in 2 teaspoons of soy sauce. Slice each inari bag diagonally to get a triangular shaped pouch. Discard the remnants. Fill the inari bags with approximately 1/8 cup of rice each and spoon in 1 teaspoon of omelet, pickled cucumber, carrot and ground chicken.

Pocket Inari

Sushi rice	2 cups
Inari	8 bags
Carrots	1 Tbsp.
Green peas	1 Tbsp.
Corn	1 Tbsp.
Cooked bay shrimp	1/2 cup
Cooking oil	2 Tbsp.
Soy sauce	4 tsp.
Salt and pepper	Dash

Makes 8 pieces

Heat 2 tablespoons of oil over medium heat. Add rice, carrots, green peas, corn and shrimp and stir fry until all the ingredients are heated through. Add soy sauce to the mixture and salt and pepper to taste. Spoon 1/4 cup rice mixture into each inari bag.

CHIRASHI

Chirashi Zushi

Chirashi zushi is another type of sushi you can easily make at home. Chirashi means "scattered" and that is exactly what chirashi zushi is - pieces of vegetables and fish decoratively scattered on a bed of rice. The choice of toppings can be seafood, vegetables or a combination of both.

The assorted colors of the toppings and the different methods they are sliced make chirashi a very attractive dish to serve. Follow the fish slicing techniques and vegetable preparation sections at the end of the book to decorate your bowl of chirashi. Serve chirashi zushi in beautiful lacquer bowls for a traditional presentation or use more modern dinnerware to highlight the rainbow colors of the toppings. If raw fish is one of the ingredients, accompany the chirashi with a small dish of soy sauce for dipping.

The varieties of toppings are endless and you are only limited by your imagination. Some traditional ingredients used are eggs, spinach, bamboo shoots, crab, eel and tuna. The following recipes are designed to give you a basic idea of what chirashi is and to stimulate your creativity.

Seafood Chirashi

Step By Step Seafood Chirashi

Seafood Chirashi

Sushi Rice 1 1/2 cup

Cooked Shrimp · Yellowtail · Salmon
Snapper · Octopus · Tuna · Surf clam · Mackerel
Uni (sea urchin) · Ikura (salmon roe) · Masago (capelin roe)
Squid · Cucumber · Radish sprouts
Shiso Leaf · Shredded nori

Makes 1 serving

Chirashi is a simple dish to make. The amount of ingredients you add to the chirashi is at your discretion. It is basically a bowl of rice with various types of seafood and vegetables scattered decoratively on top. You can use the seafood and vegetables listed on the left or create your own version, increasing or decreasing the amount of toppings according to your desire. Use the various sashimi cuts to create different styles and textures. Allow your imagination to decorate the bowl of chirashi.

1. Pre-slice all the ingredients and lay them before you to make it easier to arrange them on the rice.

2. Sprinkle the shredded nori over the rice before you layer in the seafood ingredients.

3. Use thinly sliced pieces of sashimi to create a "rose" for decoration. Refer to page 119 for tips on making a sashimi rose.

4. Continue to decorate the bowl with the remaining ingredients, covering any exposed portions of rice.

5. Make final adjustments before presentation.

Naruto Chirashi

Sushi Rice   1 cup
Eel · Salmon · Squid
Ikura (Salmon roe) · Masago (Capelin roe)
Shiso leaf · Radish sprouts · Cucumber

Makes 1 serving

Naruto is the Japanese word for "whirlpool". The squid and shiso leaf are rolled up to resemble mini whirlpools that add a playful design to this dish. After scoring the squid on one side, flip it over and lay a shiso leaf on top. Roll them together and cut into smaller sections (see page 121). Cut the eel into 1/2 inch slices and scatter them over the rice. To make the "rose" decoration, combine thinly sliced pieces of salmon and squid (see page 119). Garnish with ikura and masago.

Garden Chirashi

Sushi Rice 1 cup
Cooked shrimp
Lotus root · Snow peas · Cucumber
Asparagus · Red radish · Green onions
Sea kelp · Pickled egg plant

Makes 1 serving

The majority of ingredients in this chirashi are vegetables. If you prefer to use all vegetables, do not add shrimp but substitute in another vegetable of your choice. Refer to the vegetable preparation section for directions on cooking the lotus root, snow peas and asparagus. Thinly slice all the vegetables and arrange them as shown in the picture. Garnish with sea kelp.

OSHI ZUSHI

Oshi Zushi

Oshi zushi, or pressed sushi, comes from the Kansai style of sushi making. Cooked foods and vegetables are generally used in this style rather than raw seafood. If raw seafood intimidates your friends and family but you want to serve a traditional Japanese meal, oshi zushi is an excellent option. Rice and the ingredients of choice are pressed together in a mold to form a square or rectangular shaped sushi. After the sushi is released from the mold, it is cut into bite size pieces. Traditionally, a wooden mold (see pg. 135) is used but you can improvise with a glass baking dish or container. Remember that the vinegar in the rice will react with metal so avoid using a metallic baking pan. Try oshi zushi at your next dinner party, it is sure to impress everyone.

Shrimp Oshi Zushi

Shrimp Oshi Zushi

Shrimp Oshi Zushi

Sushi rice	2 cups
Denbu (Fish powder) flavored rice	2 cups (2 cups sushi rice mixed with 4 tablespoons of Denbu)
Cooked shrimp	18 pieces
Omelet	4 strips (8" X 2" X 1/4")
Cucumber	4 strips (8' X 2" X 1/4")
Umeshio (Pickled plum) powder	2 1/2 tablespoons
Glass baking dish	1 (8" X 8" X 2")

1. Cover the glass baking dish with a sheet of saran wrap.

2. Place a layer of shrimp across the bottom. The shrimps should be butterflied and shelled with tails removed.

3. Cover the shrimp with 2 cups of sushi rice. Press down on the rice to create an even and smooth surface.

4. Layer in the slices of omelet.

5. Add sliced cucumbers on top of the omelet.

6. Sprinkle the umeshio powder evenly over the cucumbers.

7. Spread 2 cups of the denbu flavored rice on top as the last ingredient.

8. Fold the edges of the saran wrap to cover the sushi completely.

9. Use another baking pan of the same size to press the layers of ingredients together.

10. Press down on the sushi with even weight and pressure. Look through the sides of the glass dish to make sure that all the layers have been pressed together.

11. Flip the baking dish over and gently release the sushi. Use one hand to support the sushi as it falls out of the dish.

12. Wet the blade of your knife and slice the sushi with the saran wrap still wrapped around it. The saran wrap will keep the sushi pieces together. Slice the sushi into thirds along the rows of shrimp.

13. Slice each row into smaller sections making sure to keep each piece of shrimp intact. Remove the saran wrap from each piece and serve.

SASHIMI

Sashimi

The difference between sushi and sashimi is that sashimi is served without rice. Fish, clams, octopus and other popular sushi toppings are regularly featured in sashimi. With the exception of a few items, the seafood that graces each plate is served raw. Sashimi is often served as an appetizer before the main course and accompanied with wasabi and soy sauce for dipping.

The essence of sashimi is the freshness of the seafood. If you serve sashimi, go through the trouble of buying the freshest fish and shellfish. Specialty fish markets and Asian grocery stores will carry high quality seafood reserved for sashimi, so ask for "sashimi grade" seafood. The cooking process and sauces may mask an inferior quality fish but since sashimi is served raw, it is impossible to hide any defects. Spend the extra money to buy top quality seafood, you won't regret it.

Next to freshness, presentation is the most important part of sashimi. The fish and shellfish are skillfully cut and elegantly arranged on a plate before they are served. Sashimi chefs spend years practicing slicing techniques before cutting their first piece of fish. Sharp knives are essential in making clean cuts and paper-thin slices. Use a whetstone or steel to keep your blade sharp. There are several methods of slicing fish for sashimi; tuna, yellowtail and salmon are often cut into blocks. Snapper and other white colored fish are thinly sliced as are clams and octopus. Refer to page 118 for the different cutting techniques.

The plate of sashimi is often garnished with shredded daikon or seaweed. The curly white threads of the daikon and dark color of the seaweed add contrast to the colorful pieces of sliced seafood. Shiso leaves are also common garnishes. Use your imagination and sense of style to arrange a dazzling assortment of sashimi.

Sashimi Combination

おにぎり

ONIGIRI

Onigiri

Onigiri are balls of rice molded into a variety of shapes and sizes. In some parts of Japan, they are known as onigiri and in others, they are called omusubi. For the sake of simplicity, this book will refer to them as onigiri.

There are four categories of onigiri. All of them are made with plain cooked rice and flavored in different manners to distinguish them. Filled Onigiri are flavored by a small piece of pickled vegetable hidden inside, and Grilled Onigiri are toasted over a flame to produce a crisp outer shell. Garnished Onigiri receive their flavor from the furikake seasoning, while Wrapped Onigiri are simply covered with nori or pickled leaves.

Onigiri are quick and easy to make. Japanese moms pack onigiri for their children's lunch or family picnics instead of sandwiches. The rice is molded by hand into triangles, balls and ovals and then flavored in various ways. Plastic molds can also be used and are available in fun and fancy shapes such as stars and cars. Let your imagination run free and create onigiri that will surprise and delight your children.

Onigiri are popular among adults as well. Many Japanese restaurants offer them as a side dish and patrons often substitute onigiri for the traditional bowl of rice to accompany their meal. Onigiri are extremely versatile and can be eaten for lunch, dinner or as a snack.

Onigiri Combination

Onigiri

Cooked rice   2 cups
Salt   A pinch

Makes 4 pieces

Use cooked rice instead of sushi rice (rice flavored with awasezu). The garnishes you add will provide enough flavor for the onigiri. The following steps show how to make a basic onigiri. Shape the rice with your hands or use a mold to create different shapes.

1. Wet both hands before you start.

2. Rub a small amount of salt over your hands to help flavor the rice as you mold it.

3. Scoop up 1/2 cup of rice and mold it into the desired shape. In the picture above, the chef is molding the rice into a triangular shape. You can mold it into a ball, rectangle or any shape you like.

4. Shape the rice until you are satisfied with the appearance of the onigiri. If your hands have dried during the molding process wet them again to prevent rice from sticking to them.

Onigiri (Filled)

Cooked Rice	2 cups
Takuan (pickled daikon)	4 small pieces
Roasted sesame seeds	Garnish
Black sesame seeds	Garnish
Green nori flakes	Garnish

Makes 4 pieces

Use 1/2 cup of rice for each piece of filled onigiri. Before you form the rice into the desired shape, place a small piece of takuan or other pickled vegetables in the center and mold the rice around it. The idea here is to hide a "surprise" in the middle of the rice. Garnish the outside with sesame seeds and nori flakes.

Onigiri (grilled)

Cooked Rice	2 cups
Soy sauce	2 tsp.
Miso paste	2 tsp.

Makes 4 pieces

Grilled onigiri is delicious and will most likely become your favorite. After molding the rice into the desired shape, brush the sides with soy sause or miso paste. Grill one side first. Wait until the flame has browned the whole side before flipping it over. If you flip the onigiri too early, the rice will stick to the grill and the onigiri will fall apart. You can also brown the onigiri in a pan with a little oil.

Onigiri (Garnished)

Cooked Rice	2 cups
Furikake (assorted seasonings)	1 cup

Makes 4 pieces

Combine the furikake & rice together before molding the mixture into the desired shape. To add more color or flavor garnish the outside with more furikake. Furikake comes in a myriad of flavors and colors. Choose the ones most appealing to you.

Onigiri (Wrapped)

Cooked Rice	2 cups
Nori	2 strips
Shiso leaf	1 leaf
Takana (pickled vegetables)	2 leaves

Makes 4 pieces

This type of onigiri is perhaps the simplest. The ball of rice is garnished with a piece of nori or takana. Mold the rice into the desired shape and wrap it with a strip of nori or takana. You can either wrap the whole onigiri or just a portion of it as seen in the picture.

VEGETARIAN

Vegetarian Sushi

Sushi itself is very healthy, but for those who do not like seafood or are more conscientious about their diet, vegetarian sushi is an excellent alternative. The styles and recipes in the following pages are based on traditional sushi but with some "artistic license" taken. The basics of sushi are simple; the variations are endless. Use the traditional vegetables suggested or create your own sushi with your favorites.

Some of the vegetables used in these recipes may not be familiar, but you may be able to find them at your local supermarket. If your market does not have what you are looking for, you can almost always find these vegetable in the Asian grocery stores.

The beauty of sushi lies with its colors, textures and attention to detail. Take time to plan and design a vegetarian smorgasbord for the eyes as well as the palate. The variety of colors, shapes and textures that exists in the vegetable world are endless; create a presentation that will have your friends and family singing your praises for years to come.

Vegetarian Nigiri

Sushi Rice
Shiitake mushrooms
Kampyo (dried gourd)
Asparagus
Red radish
Nori
Radish sprouts
Tofu
Inari (fried tofu pockets)
Sesame seeds
Avocado
Japanese pumpkin
Daikon radish
Carrot
Snow peas
Tomato
Cucumber
Ume paste (pickled plum)

Mold balls of rice into small blocks as you would nigiri zushi and adorn with slices of vegetables. Some vegetables must be cooked and flavored before use. Refer to the vegetable preparation section for details. (page123)

Vegetarian Roll

Sushi Rice · Nori
Cucumber · Takuan (pickled daikon)
Carrot · Japanese pumpkin · Avocado
Tomato · Asparagus · Radish sprouts · Snow peas
Spinach · Kampyo (dried gourd)
Shiitake mushrooms

Follow the same directions for making maki zushi and substitute in different kinds of vegetable for seafood. You can use any variety of vegetables you like. The ones listed on the left are just suggestions for you to follow.

Vegetarian Hand Roll

Sushi Rice · Nori · Tofu
Snow peas · Enoki mushrooms
Takuan (pickled daikon) · Black sesame seeds
Shiitake mushrooms · Kampyo (dried gourd) · Carrot
Asparagus · Roasted sesame seeds
Natto (fermented soybeans) · Cucumber
Radish sprouts · Green onion

Use the suggested vegetables on the left or your favorites to create handrolls. The combinations are endless and the only guideline is if your creation is pleasing to your palate.

Vegetarian Chirashi

Sushi Rice 1 cup
Mountain vegetables · Shiitake mushrooms
Lotus root · Carrot · Kampyo (dried gourd)
Inari (fried tofu pockets) · Sesame seeds · Bamboo shoots
Umeboshi (pickled plums) · Omelet

Garnish a bowl of rice with vegetables cut into various pattern and shapes. Use your imagination to decorate the bowl of chirashi and create a meal that is not only healthy but pleasing to the eye.

Vegetable Onigiri

Sushi Rice
Takuan (pickled daikon)
Kampyo (dried gourd) · Snow peas
Roasted sesame seeds · Carrot · Asparagus · Okra
Green peas · Blackbeans · Red beans
Green onions · Japanese pumpkin

Follow the directions for onigiri on page 94 and mix in beans and other vegetables of your choice. Form them into balls, triangles or other fun shapes. Another version of onigiri is to wrap slices of vegetables around the rice. Cut large vegetables such as carrots and takuan into thin slices lengthwise and wrap them around the ball of rice. Garnish with other vegetables.

PREPARRATION

Step By Step Rice Preparation

Washing Rice

It is always a good idea to wash the rice before cooking. Although the rice may look clean, there may be talc and dust particles mixed in that are undetectable to the naked eye. These particles will affect the taste and presentation of the cooked product.

1. Pour the measured amount of rice into a large bowl or tub.

2. Fill the bowl or tub with cold water and stir the rice with your hand. Continue stirring the rice until the water becomes cloudy.

3. Pour away the cloudy water and refill the bowl with fresh cold water.

4. Repeat this process until the water is clear and you can see the rice through the water.

5. Transfer the rice to a colander and allow the rice to drain for 1/2 hour.

Cooking Rice

If you own an electric rice cooker, follow the instructions from the manufacturer and just sit back and wait for perfectly cooked rice to magically appear. If you don't have an electric rice cooker, don't worry. Rice can be cooked in a conventional saucepan. A medium saucepan with a heavy bottom will suffice. It will just take a little more work than pushing the "on" button of the electric rice cooker.

Electric Rice Cooker

Ingredients:

Uncooked rice	2 cups
Water	2 1/2 cups

1. Transfer the washed rice from the colander to the saucepan.

2. Pour in 2 1/2 cups of water.

3. Cover the sauce-pan and boil the rice on high heat for 20 minutes. Do not remove the lid during this cooking process, the steam will help cook the rice. The lid may vibrate due to the pressure from the steam but keep the lid on at all times.

4. After the rice has cooked for 20 minutes, turn off the heat and let the pan sit covered for another 10 minutes.

5. Remove lid and transfer the rice to a mixing bowl.

Seasoning Rice

In Japanese restaurants, sushi rice is cooled and seasoned in a wooden tub called a "hangiri". The tub is shallow and has a large flat bottom designed to cool rice rapidly. In America, a hangiri may be hard to come by so any plastic or glass mixing bowl will do. Avoid using metallic or stainless steel mixing bowls as the vinegar dressing (awasezu) will react with the metal resulting in an undesirable flavor. You will also need a hand held fan (or newspaper or cardboard) to cool the rice as you mix it.

Ingredients:

Cooked rice	4 cups
AFC Natural Sushi Rice / Salad Seasoning with Vinegar	1/2 cup

1. Transfer the cooked rice to a hangiri or mixing bowl.

2. Distribute the awasezu over the rice evenly by pouring it slowly over the spatula and allowing the liquid to drip over the rice. This technique will prevent any one area from receiving too much vinegar. As you slowly pour the awasezu onto the spatula, rotate the spatula back and forth to sprinkle the vinegar dressing onto the rice.

3. Cover as much area of the rice as you can with the awasezu. After all the awasezu has been evenly distributed, use the spatula to mix the rice and awasezu together gently to avoid breaking the rice grains. Hold the spatula at a 45° angle and cut into the rice in a slicing motion. Use the spatula to lift and turn over the rice to thoroughly fold in the awasezu.

4. As you mix the rice, fan the rice to cool it down. For those who are not ambidextrous, you may require the help of another set of hands to fan the rice as you mix it.

5. After the awazesu has been thoroughly mixed in and the rice is cool enough to touch, place a cloth over the mixing bowl. This will to keep the rice from drying out until you are ready to make sushi. The rice should have a glossy sheen to it.

Step By Step # Dashi Stock

Dashi is a simple stock made with kombu and bonito flakes. This stock is used in a variety of recipes to flavor vegetables and is the base for miso soup. Kombu is a type of seaweed and requires a little preparation before it can be used. Clean the kombu by wiping off any excess dirt or sand with a wet cloth. With a pair of scissors or a knife, make some incisions to help bring out the flavor.

Ingredients:

Kombu	2 or 3 pieces (3 inches long)
Bonito flakes	one handful
Water	4 1/2 cups

(makes 4 cups of stock)

1. In a pot, add water and the kombu and allow it to stand for approximately 30 minutes.

2. Cook the kombu over medium heat and remove it just before the water comes to a boil.

3. Add in the bonito flakes and bring to a boil. Skim off and discard any foam or scum that may form during the boiling process.

4. As soon as the water comes to a boil, turn off the heat immediately and wait for the bonito flakes to sink to the bottom.

5. Remove the bonito by pouring the stock through a fine mesh colander to strain the stock. The dashi stock is now ready to use.

Selecting Seafood

Often served raw with few garnishes, if any, the seafood in sushi and sashimi is the focus of the dish. The flavor of each piece must be at its peak because there are no sauces or competing ingredients to mask an inferior product. In Japan, most sushi chefs personally visit the fresh market every morning to select the highest quality fish and seafood brought in by the fishing fleet. They go through the trouble because they know that in order to have the best tasting sushi, they must use the highest quality product. In addition to taste, presentation is also an essential part of the meal. Fresh seafood that is artistically cut and arranged provides each plate with texture, color, and brilliance that capture the attention of the diners.

In America, access to a fresh fish market is limited and most of us have to purchase seafood from the local supermarket. Many supermarkets carry high quality seafood but you may also want to visit a market that specializes in seafood. These markets have a greater selection and higher quality of fish and other seafood. The clerks at these places are often more knowledgeable about the products they carry and can inform you about which species are in season. Look for items that are labeled "Sushi or Sashimi Grade". Japanese supermarkets also carry very high quality cuts of fish and seafood. So if you are fortunate enough to live near one, it should be your first choice of places to buy seafood specifically for sushi and sashimi. The chances of getting poor quality seafood at Japanese supermarkets are slim - the sushi savy clientele that frequent the market demands only the best.

Selecting Fish

When selecting fish for your sushi or sashimi meal, keep the following in mind.

- Always buy fish that are in season.
- Most fish can be eaten raw but for health and safety reasons, choose fish that are commonly used in sushi and sashimi.
- Do not use fresh water fish because many fresh water species carry parasites that are harmful.
- The overall color of the fish should be bright or lustrous.
- Touch the fish to make sure that the flesh is firm and resilient. Stale fish are less elastic and may feel sticky.
- The eyes should be bright and clear, not sunken. The pupil should be black and unclouded.
- There should be no fishy odor, only the briny scent of the ocean.
- Check the gills. They should be bright red. Any black color around the gill indicates a stale fish.

With larger species of fish such as tuna, yellowtail and salmon, it is more convenient and economical to buy just a portion of it. Besides, you may not be able to find a whole tuna or yellowtail at the supermarket. Use the following guidelines when choosing fillets or smaller cuts.

- The color should be bright and the fillet should look moist.
- Fish with white colored flesh should look translucent.
- Tuna fillets from the belly portion should have distinct stripes while fillets from other parts should be clear red without any stripes.
- The most delicious portion of the fish is the back. With Tuna and swordfish, however, the tender portions from the belly are highly prized because of the fat content.

Other types of Seafood

Shrimp - Try to use only live shrimp. They should be active and of good color. If the shrimp are no longer alive or frozen, check the stripes to make sure that they are distinct. The stripes should not be blurred together.

Squid - Touch the tentacles and check that the suckers are still active. The skin around the eyes should be clear blue.

Shellfish - Gently pry open the shell and check to see that the shell will close by itself. Shells that remain open means that the mollusk is already dead.

Sea Urchin Roe - Only purchase roe from a source that can guarantee its freshness. The roe should be yellow or orange in color, firm and not slimy. Roe that is not fresh or have been stored too long is not worth trying.

Step By Step How to Fillet a Fish

The following are the basic steps for filleting a fish. Although the fish pictured below is rather large and the likelihood that you will fillet a fish of this size is rare, the steps for filleting a large or small fish are very similar. If you purchase your fish from a reliable fish market, you will find that the fish used for sushi and sashimi have already been filleted for you. If you prefer to fillet your own fish, however, follow the guidelines below.

1. Insert the deba-bocho or a large sharp knife into the fish slightly behind the gill and make a cut down to the chin.

2. Starting from behind the gills, cut upwards toward the top of the head.

3. Flip the fish over and repeat the same steps to sever the head.

4. The head may still be attached to the fish so use the knife to cut through any bones or flesh joining the head to the body. Once the head is removed, discard it.

5. Make an incision at the anal orifice.

6. Slice the belly open by drawing the knife in one clean stroke towards the head. The incision should be shallow to avoid puncturing the visceral organs.

7. Remove the viscera and clean the cavity with a brush under running water.

8. Make a shallow slice along the back of the fish staying close to the spine from the head to the tail.

9. Now, allow the knife to cut deep until it reaches the spine and run it along the length of the fish.

10. The cut should be deep enough so that the blade is just skimming along the spine from head to tail, severing the flesh from the spine.

11. At the tail end, cut through the skin and flesh until you reach the bone. Do not cut through the bone.

12. Slice the fish open from the tail to the anal orifice.

13. Insert the knife deeper into the tail end portion until it reaches the spine.

14. Slice along the spine from the tail to the head.

15. In smaller fish, the fillet should be separated at this point. In larger fish however, you may need to cut along the spine to completely sever the fillet.

16. Slice along the spine to separate the two halves of the fish. Cut off the tail at this point.

17. You should now have 2 fillets, one with a spine attached and one without. With your knife, remove any bones left on the fillet. You may need to use tweezers to remove the smaller bones.

18. Clean the belly area of the fillet by cutting away any excess skin.

19. Repeat the fillet process with the other half of the fish. Make a shallow incision along the spine first then cut deep into the fish staying close to the spine.

20. Remove the fins from the fillet

21. Start with one fillet and cut it into smaller, more manageable portions.

22. Slice the fillet into two sections lengthwise along the spine separating the belly from the back.

23. In larger fish, the area around the spine will contain bones and dark flesh that has been colored by blood. Cut and discard the darker portions.

24. Most fish that cruise the open ocean such as tuna and yellowtail have two toned musculature. Discard the dark color muscle. Avoid using the dark portions of the flesh. They should not be used for sashimi and nigiri.

25. After the dark colored flesh has been trimmed away, slice the fillet horizontally into smaller blocks. Cut the fish into more manageable rectangular blocks, so that it will be easier for you to slice the fish for sashimi and nigiri zushi.

26. Skin the fish by inserting the blade between the flesh and the skin starting at the tail end. With your left hand (assuming you are holding the knife in your right hand), pull the skin away in a gentle sawing motion while keeping the knife stationary. Keep the knife at a slight angle and tight to the skin allowing the blade to separate the flesh form the skin. Repeat with the other fillet.

Step By Step Fish Slicing Techniques

According to sushi connoisseurs, how a piece of fish is sliced affects the way it tastes. Apprentices spend years mastering fish cutting techniques before graduating to become sushi chefs. Cutting techniques vary from fish to fish depending on its species and it is up to the chef to make each slice visually and texturally attractive. The prowress of a chef is determined by how skillfully he slices his ingredients.

The following are some basic techniques used in sushi and sashimi. The long, slender blade of the sashimi bocho is used to slice fish after it has been filleted. One of the basics in sushi and sashimi cutting is that each cut should be in one swift motion. Never saw the fish back and forth. A sawing motion will leave the piece of fish with a ragged edge, compromising the appearance and taste. In order to slice through the fish in one motion, the knife you use must be extremely sharp. It is always a good idea to sharpen the blade each time before slicing fish.

Angle cut for sushi and sashimi

Begin with a small block approximately the width of your hand (3 inches across and 1 1/2 inches high) cut from a larger portion of fish. There should be no problem trimming off a smaller portion from large fish such as tuna and yellowtail. The shape of the block will help in producing uniform slices. Smaller species of fish, however, will be more challenging to slice since you will not have a symmetrical block to start off from. Cut the fish into slices by following the angle of the fillet. The more parallel the blade is to the cutting board, the wider the slice of fish.

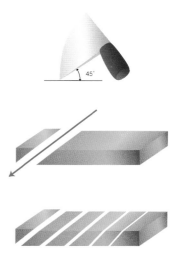

1. Measure about 1 1/2 inches in from the top and slice off a piece from the top down towards the bottom corner in a 45° angle. The result should be a triangular piece and the original block with a slanted surface.

2. Angle your knife to match the working edge of the block and cut a slice by pulling the blade towards you in one swift motion. The slice of fish should be about 1/4 inch in thickness.

3. Repeat this process maintaining the knife at a 45° angle for all of the slices. The last piece should also be a triangular wedge similar to the very first piece. These end pieces can be chopped up and used in maki zushi.

Sashimi cut

Besides the angle cut, there are two other basic techniques used in sashimi. The different types of cuts create different shapes and sizes, making the sashimi platter more beautiful and interesting.

Straight cut - In the straight cut technique, simply cut straight down on a block of fish at a 90° angle. Make sure that each piece is approximately 1/4 inch in thickness and that the sides are straight, resembling a miniature block. Each piece should be no more than 2 inches in length.

Paper-thin cuts - Paper-thin cuts are used exclusively for white colored fish. It is the same technique as the angle cut only that the slices are even thinner - 1/8 inch thick. Each slice should be translucent. With most white colored fish, the fillets are much thinner and are more difficult to cut. For thinner fillets or blocks, reduce the angle of the knife to get larger slices. Instead of slicing at a 45° angle, try a 30° or 35° angle to achieve the desired result.

Fish-rose

1. Cut slices of fish approximately 1/8 inch or thinner.

2. Angle the knife and cut the fish at a 30° angle to get a thin, almost transparent slice. The more parallel the knife is to the table, the thinner and wider the piece of fish will be.

3. Cut off 3 slices and wrap them around each other to form a rose.

Step By Step # Shellfish

Shrimp (Ebi)

1. Without peeling it, devein the shrimp with a bamboo skewer. Push a bamboo skewer through the shrimp bet-ween the shell and flesh along the belly underside of the shrimp. The bamboo skewer will keep the shrimp from curling up when cooked.

2. Boil the shrimp until the color changes to red.

3. Remove the skewer and peel the shrimp leaving the tail.

4. Butterfly the shrimp by slicing it along the belly from head to tail.

5. The shrimp is now ready to be used in a variety of sushi (dishes).

Surf Clam (Hokkigai)

1. Butterfly the clam by slicing it in half.

2. Rinse away any dirt that is inside the clam. Pat dry with paper towels.

3. Cut off the end of the clam.

Sweet Shrimp (Amaebi)

1. Cut off the head and discard. Peel the shell off leaving the tail portion intact.

2. Butterfly the shrimp by slicing along the back ending at the tail.

3. Remove the vein. The shrimp is now ready as a topping for nigiri zushi.

Decorative Squid Sashimi

Score the squid fillet with a knife to create an interesting pattern. Cut a piece of nori the same size as the fillet and lay it on top. The scored side should be facing down on the cutting board. Place several strips of carrots at one end and roll the squid and nori together. Cut the roll into sections.

121

Step By Step Vegetable Cutting Techniques

Wide slice
Cut vegetables such as cucumber, carrots and takuan lengthwise to achieve a long, wide slice. These slices are used to make vegetarian nigiri or to form layers in oshi zushi.

Thick Strips
Vegetables cut into strips approximately 1/4 inch thick are used in maki zushi. Cucumbers, carrots and takuan are common examples cut in this fashion.

Julienne
To create a different look for maki zushi, you may prefer to use julienned vegetables instead of the thick strips. Cut the vegetables into 1/8 inch thickness or use a mandolin for consistency.

Match Sticks
Match stick cuts are a little thinner than julienne cuts and much shorter. This type of cut is used in vegetarian sushi.

Dice
Finely diced vegetables are seldom used in sushi preparation other than to flavor and add color to rice. Rice mixed with vegetables can be used for inari or chirashi zushi.

Slice
Vegetables with large surface areas such as lotus root and carrots are always thinly sliced. Each slice should be no more than 1/4 inch in thickness. Serve them as they are or cut them into decorative patterns with garnish cutters.

Snow peas Remove the strings from the snow peas before cooking them. You may leave the ends intact if you like. Cut the snow peas into smaller peices or into thin strips.

Avocados Avocados are always sliced before use. Each quarter of the avocado can be sliced into 3-4 pieces depending on the size of the avocado.

Step By Step Shiitake

Shiitake Mushrooms	
Shiitake mushrooms	6
Water (for soaking mushrooms)	2 cups
Sugar	2 Tbsp.
Sake	2 Tbsp.
Soy sauce	3 Tbsp.
Mirin	1 Tbsp.

1. Soak the mushrooms in a bowl of water until soft, approximately 20 minutes.

2. Cut off the stems and place mushrooms into a pot with the rest of the ingredients except for the mirin.

3. Cook the mushrooms until most of the liquid has evaporated. Add in the mirin to give the mushroom a glossy sheen.

4. Remove mushrooms from the heat and allow them to cool. Slice the mushrooms into fine strips.

Step By Step Spinach

1. Add spinach to a boiling pot of water.

2. Remove the spinach as soon as it wilts.

3. Rinse under cold water to stop the cooking process.

4. Dry the spinach by squeezing out the water.

5. Cut off the roots.

Step By Step Lotus Root (Renkon)

Lotus Root

Lotus root	150 g
Dashi stock	2 cups
Soy sauce	1 Tbsp.

1. Peel away the outer skin of the lotus root.

2. Cut the root into thin 1/8inch slices.

3. Place the sliced lotus root into bowl of water with a small amount of vinegar. The vinegar will keep the lotus root from oxidizing and turning brown.

4. Boil the root in dashi for 5 minutes or until tender. Add in soy sauce and boil for 1 minute more.

5. When the lotus root is cooked, strain it through a colander.

Step By Step Burdock (Gobo)

Burdock

Burdock	40 g
Dashi	2 cups
Soy Sauce	1 Tbsp.

1. Wash the burdock thoroughly with a brush. Scrape off the outer skin with a knife. Do not peel.

2. Make 6 shallow incisions in equal intervals around the burdock.

3. Shave the burdock to create thin flakes and soak them in a bowl of water and vinegar. The vinegar will keep it from turning brown. When you are ready to cook the burdock, drain the water and boil it in dashi and soy sauce. Boil it until soft, approximately 5 minutes.

Step By Step Dried Gourd Shavings (Kampyo)

Dried Gourd

Dried gourd	20 g
Dashi stock	2 cups
Salt	1/4 tsp.
Sugar	1 1/2 Tbsp.
Soy sauce	1 1/2 Tbsp.
Mirin	1 1/2 Tbsp.

1. Soak the gourd in water for 5 minutes.

2. Pour away the water and rub the gourd with a small amount of salt. Wash the salt away and squeeze the gourd dry.

3. In a pot, combine the gourd, dashi stock, soy sauce and sugar together. Cook over medium heat until the liquid has evaporated.

Step By Step Garnish

Garnishes add to the appeal of sushi and are used to decorate and embellish the final product. Most of the garnishes used are either finely grated, chopped or shredded. Follow the examples below to create garnishes to decorate your sushi.

Daikon To create the fluffy white garnish used in sashimi, remove the outer skin of the daikon. Pare it as you would the skin of an apple and roll the piece together tightly. Then slice it into thin strips. The strips contain a lot of liquid and are extremely limp at this point. Place them in a bowl of cold water to make them firm and curly.

Green onions Green onions or scallions are sliced very thin as pictured. Both the leaves and the stalk are used in decorating sushi but it is usually the green portion that is finely chopped. The white portion are cut into thin strips.

Ginger Use a cheese grater or any other kind of graters with fine teeth to grate the ginger. Raw ginger is always grated, never sliced.

Omelet

Eggs	3
Dashi stock	2 Tbsp.
Sugar	2 Tbsp.
Salt	1/4 tsp.

You can use any pan to make the omelet but a rectangular one is very helpful in forming the shape. A non-stick pan will also make the process easier and reduce the amount of oil used.

1. Immerse a paper towel in cooking oil and use it to coat the surface of the pan with oil.

2. Drop a small amount of the egg mixture into the pan. When it sizzles, the pan is hot enough to start cooking the omelet.

3. Pour 1/3 of the egg mixture into the pan.

4. When the egg mixture has set, start at the far end of the pan and fold the egg mixture towards you. Fold the omelet at 2-inch intervals, forming a block that is approximately 2 inches wide when you finish.

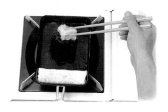

5. Grease the pan again with the paper towel.

6. Push the first layer to the far end of the pan before you add more of the egg mixture to the pan.

7. Pour in 1/2 of the remaining egg mixture.

8. Lift the first layer to make sure that the egg mixture coats the pan underneath it.

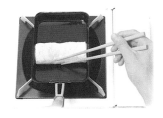

9. When the egg mixture has solidified, fold the layers together at 2-inch intervals and push the omelet towards the far end. Repeat the same steps with the last portion of egg mixture.

10. When the omelet is completely cooked, remove it from the pan and place it on the makisu.

11. While the omelet is still hot, use the makisu to adjust the shape.

12. Leave the omelet in the makisu and secure the ends with rubber bands to hold the form. Remove the omelet from the makisu when it has cooled.

Fish / Seafood Ingredients

Scallops (Hotate)

Scallops are served raw as well as cooked at the sushi bar. They come in two sizes, large pieces are served as nigiri zushi and the smaller pieces are served gunkan style. Some sushi chefs broil the scallops with a little mayonnaise and masago sauce, an option worth trying at home.

Salmon (Sake)

The vibrant orange color of the salmon makes it one of the most attractive fish. Salmon is used as an ingredient for all types of sushi and sashimi. You can serve it raw, smoked or grilled. Go to a reliable fish market to get the highest quality salmon.

Yellowtail (Hamachi)

Hamachi or yellowtail is one of the most popular items served at the sushi bar. The light colored meat and buttery flavor is a favorite among sushi lovers. Most of the yellowtails served in the United States are imported from Japan where they are grown in hatcheries and harvested when they reach 15-20 pounds.

Red Snapper (Tai)

Tai or red snapper is another common item at the sushi bar. Although the fish the Japanese call tai is not available in the United States, the red snapper is a good substitute because of the similarity in taste and texture. The pink and white flesh has a slight resistance to the bite and is delicious when served with ponzu (citrus-soy) sauce.

Crab (Kani)

Alaskan king crab or snow crab can be used to make nigiri zushi or maki zushi. Crab is always served cooked. The flesh from the legs is the most suitable in terms of color, texture and appearance. Crab can be used as a substitute for imitation crab in the California Roll.

Squid (Ika)

Squid is a shellfish that is commonly served in sushi bars. Before serving, you should score the squid to tenderize it and give the soy sauce something to cling to. Squid is often called calamari in the supermarkets but the squid served in the sushi bars is from a species native to Japan.

Imitation Crab Sticks (Kanikama)

Kanikama is the Japanese name for imitation crab sticks and is the main ingredient in California Rolls. This product is cooked and can be eaten as is. Most supermarkets carry this product but if you can't find it, ask the seafood manager - he may know it as "Surimi".

Tuna (Maguro)

Tuna is probably the most popular fish in the sushi bar. Not only is the flesh soft and mild in flavor, it freezes well, so there is always an abundant supply in the sushi case. The unmistakable deep red color of the tuna makes a beautiful presentation as nigiri zushi or sashimi. The quality of tuna is consistent all year round but the best is during the winter season between November and February. There are many species of tuna but the ones most commonly used in the United States are blue fin and yellow fin tuna. The most sought after part of the tuna is the meat from the belly area. This part of the fish is called "toro" and is usually the most expensive item at the sushi bar. It is extremely tender because of the high fat content and has a rich buttery flavor - well worth the price.

Salmon Roe (Ikura)

Ikura is one of the most popular items at the sushi bar because most people are familiar with it. It is often used as garnish in many western dishes and is also known as red caviar. Compared with masago, ikura is much larger, about the size of a small pea. The flavor is also more intense and saltier than masago.

Octopus (Tako)

The purple color and interesting shape of the suctions make the octopus tentacle a beautiful addition to any sushi platter. Octopus is always served cooked and thinly sliced in nigiri zushi and sashimi. Its flavor is light and not at all overpowering. The texture is a little chewy, so novice sushi patrons may need to get accustomed to it.

Surf Clam (Hokigai)

Hokigai or surf clam is a standard sushi topping available at all sushi bars. The clam is cooked and butterflied before it is served as a topping for nigiri zushi. Hokigai is a topping that can be used in chirashi zushi as well.

Sea urchin roe (Uni)

Uni may be the least appealing in terms of aesthetics but sushi connoisseurs often name uni as their favorite sushi. Uni is sea urchin roe and has almost no shape or form. It is mustard yellow in color and is often served in the gunkan style. Fresh uni has a subtle nutlike flavor but once frozen, it loses it flavor.

Denbu and Bonito Flakes

Denbu (left) is a powder that is made from fish and used primarily in Futomaki. Bonito flakes are shavings from a species of fish called bonito, and come in large or small flakes. The large flakes are primarily used to make dashi while the small flakes are used to garnish sushi. Asian groceries stores are your best bet for finding this item.

Shrimp (Ebi)

Shrimp is always served cooked and peeled. The familiar red and white flesh is a treat for sushi beginners timid about eating raw fish. Amaebi or sweet shrimp however, is a delicacy that is served raw. This prized topping is almost transparent in color and has a sweet flavor - well worth the high price charged at the sushi bar.

Salt Water Eel (Unagi) / Fresh Water (Anago)

Unagi is roasted freshwater eel while anago is roasted sea eel. Both types of eel are always served cooked with a sweet dark sauce. At the sushi bars, the chefs often broil the eel and serve it lightly toasted to the customer.
Unagi and anago are great introductory items for people who have never tried sushi before or are resistant to raw fish.

Mackerel (Saba)

Saba or mackerel is extremely flavorful and may be too intimidating to the sushi novice. Many connoisseurs enjoy this fish that is marinated before it is served. Mackerel is a common fish in the United States but the mackerel served in the sushi bars is imported from Japan.

Capelin Roe (Masago)

Capelin is a kind of smelt and its roe is used in many recipes. The bright orange of the masago lends a beautiful color to sushi and is often used in different kinds of maki sushi, hand rolls, chirash and gunkan zushi. Masago has a slight resistance to the bite and is salty in flavor.

Vegetables and other ingredients

Inari

Inari is fried tofu that has been cooked in soy sauce and mirin. Some manufacturers pre-cut the inari to form little pouches. If the inari you purchase have not been cut, slice open one of the longer sides to form a pouch. Inari can be found in most Asian grocery stores.

Egg

Eggs are popular sushi ingredients. Use eggs to make the Japanese omelet for nigiri zushi and oshi zushi or shred them to garnish chirashi zushi. See page (126) for instructions on making the Japanese omelet.

Daikon

Daikon is a giant white radish that is often shredded and used as garnish for sashimi. It is eaten raw and is used in making some vegetarian sushi. Before using daikon, peel away the outer skin as you would a carrot.

Avocado

Avocado is not traditionally used in making sushi but the California Roll has popularized this fruit in the American sushi bars. Now, avocados are used in making a variety of rolls, hand rolls and vegetarian sushi. Avoid using overly ripe avocados as they will loose their shape especially under the pressure of rolling and forming the sushi.

Beans

Beans will add color and texture to your vegetable onigiri. You can use either red, black or soybeans. Keep in mind that they need to be cooked before adding them to the rice. Beans are common ingredients in vegetarian sushi but seldom used in other types of sushi.

Takuan

Takuan is a pickled daikon that has a sweet refreshing flavor. Its bright yellow color contrasts well with the white of the rice and is often used as an ingredient in maki zushi. Takuan, a fairly common item, is available at the Asian grocery stores.

Lotus Root (Renkon)

The chances of finding lotus root in your local supermarket are pretty slim so this is one item that you will need to visit the Asian grocery store for. Before the lotus root can be used, the outer layer of skin must be pared away. Similar to apples, the lotus root flesh oxidizes and turns brown very quickly. To avoid this, soak the lotus root in a vinegar solution after you have sliced it.

Cucumber

Cucumbers are often used in making a variety of sushi. Depending on your preference, you can either cut the cucumber into quarter inch thick strips or julienne style. The seeds are always discarded but the outer skin can be left on if desired.

Pickled Vegetables

Pickled vegetables have a sweet and tangy flavor that contrasts well with rice. There are many different types of pickled vegetables available at Asian grocery stores that can be used in making sushi and onigiri. Pickled vegetables can also be served as an appetizer.

Edamame

Edamame are soybeans that have been blanched in salt water. They are served in their pods and are eaten as appetizers. You can find edamame in the frozen vegetable section or the frozen Asian foods section of your supermarket.

Kampyo (Dried Gourd Shaving)

Kampyo has to be boiled in water until soft before it can be used. You can use Kampyo as a decorative tie on pieces of nigiri zushi or as an ingredient in Chirashi zushi. Kampyo is white in color. To give it additional flavor and color, cook in a soy sauce solution.

Spinach

Spinach is one of the main ingredients in Futomaki. Parboil the spinach and remove it from the water as soon as it wilts. Remove excess water and add it to your Futomaki.

Alfalfa Sprouts

Alfalfa sprouts are not traditionally used in Japanese cooking but are popular among vegetarians. Try alfalfa sprouts in your vegetarian sushi and as garnishes for your hand rolls.

Kaiware

Kaiware are the sprouts of the daikon. These sprouts are used extensively to garnish and add flavor to all the varieties of sushi. Kaiware has a slightly spicy flavor and tastes similar to the red radish.

Wasabi

You probably will not be able to find fresh wasabi root in the United States but if you do, this is how to prepare freshly grated wasabi. With a knife, scrape away the outer skin, do not pare it as you would a carrot or a potato. After the rough outer skin has been scraped away, use a fine grater to grate the wasabi. Only scrape away the skin of the portion you intend to use as the wasabi will quickly lose its flavor without the protection of the skin. Refrigerate any leftover portion. You can purchase wasabi from your Asian grocery store in powder form or in tubed packages.

Konbu

Konbu is a large seaweed that is primarily used to flavor dashi stock. Most of the konbu sold in the United States are dried and will have to be soaked in water before use. Score the konbu to release more flavor into the stock. You can find dried konbu in Asian grocery stores.

Seaweed

Seaweed comes in a variety of colors and shapes. They are high in vitamins and minerals and have always been an important part of the Japanese diet. Seaweed can be used as a garnish or as one of the main ingredients of the dish. Packages of dried seaweed are available at Asian grocery stores.

Furikake

Furikake is a delicious seasoning for rice. It comes in a variety of flavors but usually has sesame seeds, roasted seaweed and bonito flakes as the main ingredients. Sprinkle this seasoning on cooked rice or roll your onigiri in it for different colors and flavor. Furikake can be found in the Asian section of your supermarket but you will find a larger selection at your local Asian grocery store.

Radish

The red and white colors of the radish make beautiful garnishes for sushi. Parboil slices of radish and create attractive vegetarian sushi.

Vegetables and other ingredients

Shiitake Mushrooms

Your supermarket may carry fresh shiitake mushrooms but they are usually sold dried. Before using, soak them in water until they become soft. Remove the stems and cook the mushrooms in a soy sauce solution.

Bamboo Shoot

Bamboo shoot is an interesting ingredient that will add distinct flavor and crisp texture to your chirashi zushi. Although it is commonly used in chirashi zushi, you may use it when making vegetarian sushi as well. You can find the bamboo shoot in sealed packages or canned. The bamboo shoots need to be cooked in dashi stock before it can be used.

Enoki Mushrooms

Enoki mushrooms are long, slender, white colored mushrooms. They are mild in flavor and are often used in a variety of Japanese dishes. Parboil the mushrooms before using to garnish sushi. Enoki mushrooms are very common and can be found in most supermarkets.

Tofu

Tofu comes in three different grades of texture-soft, medium and hard. Although you can use all three in making sushi, we recommend using medium texture. Soft tofu is very difficult to handle and can easily disintegrate in your hands if you are not careful. The hard tofu is easy to work with but the texture is a little resistant to the bite and does not have the soft, creamy characteristic normally associated with tofu.

Snow Peas

Remove the strings from the snow peas but you may leave the tops intact if you like. To get the intense green color, drop the snow peas into a pot of boiling water. As soon as the color changes from a light green to a deep green, remove the snow peas from the water. You can cut the peas diagonally into pieces or leave them whole.

Carrots

Carrots are either parboiled or marinated in sushi vinegar before they are used in making sushi. Depending on the type of sushi you are making, carrots are cut into julienne strips or sliced paper thin. You can also use molds to cut carrots into different shapes to garnish your sushi platters.

Sesame Seeds

There are two types of sesame seeds - black and white. Toast the seeds to bring out their flavor before using them to garnish your inside-out California Roll or your onigiri. White sesame seeds are readily available at the supermarket but you may need to visit an Asian grocery store for the black ones.

Asparagus

Asparagus are never eaten raw, so parboil them before using them as ingredients for your sushi. If the stalks of the asparagus are too thick, halve the asparagus lengthwise. Usually only the top portion and the tips of the asparagus are used.

Sauces

The most common sauces used in Japanese cooking are mirin (left), rice vinegar (top) and soy sauce (right). Mirin is sweet in flavor and is one of the ingredients used in preparing vegetables for sushi. Rice vinegar is milder than the other types of vinegar. The delicate flavor gives the sushi rice a unique taste. Soy sauce is used in cooking as well as a dipping sauce for sushi. A high quality soy sauce will definitely increase the enjoyment of your sushi meal.

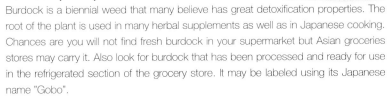

Burdock (Gobo)

Burdock is a biennial weed that many believe has great detoxification properties. The root of the plant is used in many herbal supplements as well as in Japanese cooking. Chances are you will not find fresh burdock in your supermarket but Asian groceries stores may carry it. Also look for burdock that has been processed and ready for use in the refrigerated section of the grocery store. It may be labeled using its Japanese name "Gobo".

Gari

Pickled ginger or "gari" in Japanese is served with every sushi meal. The ginger acts as a palate cleanser and is eaten between each serving of sushi. Most of the gari served in restaurants is pink in color because of food coloring that has been added but natural pickled ginger is also available.

Umeboshi

Umeboshi are pickled plums that are often used as a filling ingredient for onigiri/omusubi. It can be found in its original form, packaged in a tube or in powder form. The tangy flavor of umeboshi is a favorite among many Japanese.

Shiso

If you frequent sushi bars and Japanese restaurants, you will find that the shiso leaf is a common garnish in sashimi and sushi. In fact, shiso can also be eaten. It has a peppery taste and may be a little foreign to the American palate.

Nori

Nowadays, most supermarkets carry nori (roasted seaweed) in the Asian/International Foods section. Your local Asian grocery store however, will probably have the best selection. The highest quality of nori is black in color but the less expensive green variety can also be used in sushi making. Nori comes in several forms - sheets of 8 x 8 inches (for maki zushi), paper thin shreds (for chirashi zushi) and powder (for garnish).

Pumpkin

The pumpkin pictured here is of an Asian variety but you may use the more familiar orange ones as well. After peeling away the outer skin and discarding the seeds, the pumpkin flesh needs to be cooked in a dashi broth before it can be used.

Utensils

Square omelet pan

Use this pan to make tamago zushi. The rectangular shape makes it easy to form the egg into layers. You can also use a round omelet pan and just trim the sides of the omelet into a rectangular shape.

Colander

Colanders are generally used to drain the rice after washing. A metal colander with a fine mesh will keep the small rice grains from falling out during the draining process.

Grater

You can use any common grater to grate fresh wasabi, ginger or daikon. Make sure it can produce a fine grate as most garnishes in Japanese cuisines are extremely fine.

Fan

Sushi chefs use hand held fans to cool the rice as they mix in the vinegar solution. By cooling the rice rapidly, the vinegar clings to the rice and gives it a glossy sheen. If you do not have a fan, you can use a piece of cardboard or folded newspaper as substitutes.

Hangiri and Spatula

The Japanese use this wooden tub to cool rice and mix in awasezu. The broad bottom provides a large surface area for the rice to cool quickly and the low sides make it easy to mix the rice. The wood absorbs excess water from the rice and helps give the rice its proper texture and gloss. Before using the hangiri, soak it in water and wipe dry with a clean towel. Season the hangiri with 3 tablespoons of vinegar before adding the rice. If you do not have a hangiri, you can use any large non-metalic bowl.

Whetstone

Sushi knives need to be extremely sharp so that they can slice cleanly through fish and sushi. A dull knife will result in torn and jagged edges thus compromising the beauty of the piece of food. Always sharpen your knives before use.

Makisu

The bamboo mat is indispensible in rolling sushi. It will aid in rolling as well as forming the sushi into the shape you desire. The mat is flat on one side with ridges on the other. Always place the side with ridges on the table so that the flat side is facing up towards you. For easier clean up, cover the makisu with plastic wrap to keep rice from sticking to it.

Molds

Most experienced chefs prefer to use their hands to mold rice into the desire shaped for nigiri, and onigiri. If your skills have not been refined yet, you can always rely on plastic molds to give you the perfect shape every time. Plastic molds come in a variety of shapes and sizes. If the local Asian grocery store does not carry them, you may need to search for them in a Japanese department store or supermarket.

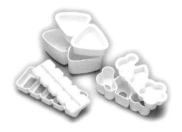

Garnish Cutters

These metallic cutters are excellent for creating beautiful shapes to garnish your sushi platter. The cutters come in a variety of shapes and sizes - you are only limited by your imagination as to the beautiful designs you can create.

Grill

A small grill will come in handy when you want to make grilled onigiri. Brush the grill with oil before placing the onigiri on top. Allow the onigiri to cook thoroughly before flipping it over to grill the other side. Pulling the onigiri off the grill before it is done will cause the rice to stick and may tear the onigiri apart.

Tweezer(s)

Tweezers come in handy when you want to remove tiny bones from the fish you filleted.

Wooden Mold

This wooden mold is traditionally used in making oshi zushi (pressed sushi). Rice, seaweed and other ingredients are layered in and pressed to form the symmetrical shapes of oshi zushi. A cake or bread pan will work just as well. Line the pan with saran wrap to keep the rice from sticking to it.

Chopsticks

Chopsticks are extremely versatile and are used for picking up pieces of food, stirring and mixing. Learning to use chopsticks may be a challenge in the beginning but after you have mastered using them, they become indispensable tools in the kitchen - especially for picking up finely chopped or diced garnishes.

Knives

Using a Japanese sashimi knife will give the best results when cutting fish into cubes and slices. Japanese knives, unlike their western counterparts, are sharpened on only one side of the blade and cut faster and cleaner than a double edge blade. The two most common type of knives used by sushi chefs are the sashimi bocho and the deba bocho.

Sashimi Bocho

The long bladed knife pictured on top is used to cut fish into slices and cubes for sashimi and sushi. The fish is cut in one swift stroke, never sawed back and forth.

Deba Bocho

The bottom knife is primarily used to fillet fish. The blade is heavy and the Japanese rely on it to cut through bones and skin.

AFC History

Advanced Fresh Concepts Corporation

Advanced Fresh Concepts Corporation (AFC) is the realization of a dream to introduce packaged sushi prepared fresh daily to America. As a child, company president and founder, Ryuji Ishii, enjoyed the convenience of packaged sushi on every street corner in his native Japan. When he moved to the United States, however, this luxury was no where to be found. Packaged sushi was virtually unheard of; not to mention sushi prepared fresh daily by a chef in the local supermarket. Determined to recreate his childhood memories and to introduce a quick, convenient and healthy fast food to the American market, Ishii embarked on a course to make sushi readily available. He opened his first supermarket sushi bar in Southern California in November of 1986.

The concept of a sushi bar in a supermarket was an instant success with Southern California residents and within a couple of years AFC had expanded its program into several local supermarket chains. News of the success of sushi circulated among circles of supermarket executives and by 1991, AFC opened its first sushi bar outside of California with a major chain in Texas. As mainstream America embraced sushi, AFC has grown into the largest and most successful sushi company today with over 900 sushi bars in 46 states and Canada.

Consumers from Alaska to Florida elevated sushi from a "California Fad" to a coveted part of their diet once they discovered its delectable flavor and nutritional value. What was once a foreign and appalling idea is now a celebrated product that consumers look for in their supermarkets. AFC is pleased to supply freshly made sushi to supermarkets and strives to constantly enhance each customer's sushi experience with premium quality ingredients and innovative new products. In addition to new varieties of sushi, AFC continues to diversify its menu by offering soba and udon (Japanese noodles), salad dressings, various appetizers and condiments to accompany each sushi meal.

Sushi Related Products

In addition to sushi, AFC offers a extensive line of premium quality sushi related products. Most are natural, without preservatives, additives and MSG (monosodium glutamate).

These products can be used in making sushi or to accompany any sushi meal. You can find the following products at your local AFC Sushi Bar or at our website- www.afcsushi.com.

Reduced Sodium Soy Sauce

AFC's tamari soy sauce has 25% less sodium than ordinary soy sauce and is excellent for dipping sushi and sashimi. Wheat is a major ingredient in most soy sauces but tamari soy sauce is made with either a very small amount of wheat or none at all. This method of brewing results in an exceptionally smooth soy sauce that can be used as a marinade for barbecues or as a seasoning for steaks, stir fry and salad dressings.

Grated Sushi Wasabi

Most brands of wasabi on the market today mix in horseradish, but AFC's grated sushi wasabi is made from 100% genuine Japanese wasabi. After harvesting, the wasabi is grated and tubed immediately to keep the flavor fresh and potent.

Natural Sushi Rice / Salad Seasoning with Vinegar

AFC's special blend of seasonings will give your rice the authentic taste you find at the sushi bars. This product is made with all natural ingredients and can be used as a substitute for vinegar in salad dressings.

Natural Sesame Seeds

Sesame seeds are used widely in Asian cooking. AFC's sesame seeds are roasted lightly to bring out the full flavor of the sesame seeds. Use this as a garnish for your sushi or try it with stir-fry, sweet and sour sauces and other favorite dishes.

Natural Green Tea

Green tea is a customary beverage served with sushi. AFC's Natural Green Tea comes from the same blend of tea commonly served in premier sushi restaurants. Each box contains 16 individually sealed tea bags.

Natural Sushi Seaweed

AFC has selected and packaged premium quality seaweed for home use. The seaweed is lightly toasted and in addition to sushi, it can be used for tempura, cold soba noodle and mixed rice. After opening, seal the package tightly and store in the refrigerator to keep dry.

Natural Miso Soup

The smooth and delicious flavor of miso soup will compliment any meal. Miso is made from soybeans and is a great source of protein, vitamins and minerals. AFC has packaged this traditional soup in individual portions that can be taken conveniently anywhere. Just add hot water and enjoy.

Natural Miso Soup with Tofu

Also packaged in ready to go containers, this version of miso soup has bits of tofu, wakame seaweed and green onions. It has the same great miso taste as its predecessor but with garnishes to add extra flavor and texture.

Natural Sushi Wasabi Powder

AFC's wasabi powder contains neither preservatives, food colors nor artificial flavors. To retain the freshness and potency the wasabi root is washed, ground into powder and immediately freeze-dried. It is also a great substitute for mustard.

Pickled Ginger

Pickled ginger or "gari" is always served at the sushi bar. Eat a piece between tasting different types of sushi to cleanse and prepare your palate for the next selection. The sweet and intense flavor of the ginger is delicious and refreshing.

Teriyaki Sauce

The sweetness of the teriyaki sauce enhances the flavors of meats, fish and vegetables. Use it as a marinade for barbecues, basting sauce for roasts or dipping sauce for cooked meats and vegetables.

Wasabi Salad Dressing

Made from grated wasabi, this dressing will add spice and zest to any salad. If you like wasabi, you'll love this dressing. AFC's Wasabi Dressing can be used as a marinade or dipping sauce as well.

Soba Tea

The Japanese have enjoyed the refreshing flavor and health benefits of soba tea for centuries. It is rich in rutin and is believed to help in lowering blood pressure. This product is the first of its kind in the United States and is only available from AFC. Add honey and lemon to make a refreshing ice tea for the hot summer days.

All Natural Miso Paste

Make miso soup at home with AFC's Miso Paste. Just dissolve the paste in hot water and you will have a nutritious and delicious soup in no time. The miso paste is made from all natural ingredients and does not contain any MSG.

Natural garnish for Miso Soup

Get all the garnishes for miso soup in one convenient bag. The package is resealable so you can use as little or as much as you want. AFC's instant garnish contains tofu, wakame seaweed, green onions and fried tofu. Add to hot soup before serving.

Ginger Salad Dressing

Liven up your salad with the exotic and intense flavor of AFC's Ginger Dressing. This versatile dressing can be used to flavor stir-fry dishes or as a marinade for barbecues. The ginger dressing also compliments the delicate flavor of fish and poultry.

Sushi Rice

Short or medium grain white rice is the most suitable for making sushi. AFC has selected a high quality blend of rice that is moist, aromatic and flavorful when cooked. Rice is the most important ingredient in sushi; choosing the highest quality rice will give you the best results.

The Ultimate Sushi Kit

Whether you are cooking for yourself or throwing a "sushi party", you will find all the necessary ingredients and condiments in the Ultimate Sushi Kit. The sushi kit is convenient and has an easy to follow instruction booklet on making sushi. Perfect for the home or as a gift.

INDEX

NOTE

NOTE